TO:

···•┊────────────────────────────────────┊•···

FROM:

···•┊────────────────────────────────────┊•···

DATE:

···•┊────────────────────────────────────┊•···

FRIENDS WITH GOD
DEVOTIONS
FOR KIDS

54 Delightfully Fun Ways to Grow Closer
to Jesus, Family, and Friends

Written by Mikal Keefer

Illustrated by David Harrington

LIFETREE

Group

LIFETREE
KIDS

Visit **MyLifetree.com/Kids** for more fun, faith-building stuff for kids!

Friends With God Devotions for Kids
54 Delightfully Fun Ways to Grow Closer to Jesus, Family, and Friends

Copyright © 2017 Group Publishing, Inc. | 0000 0001 0362 4853
Lifetree™ is an imprint of Group Publishing, Inc.

Visit our website: group.com

Credits

Author: Mikal Keefer

Illustrator: David Harrington

Chief Creative Officer: Joani Schultz

Creative Director: Michael Paustian

Lead Designer: Stephen Caine

Assistant Editor: Ann Diaz

Scripture quotations are taken from the Holy Bible, New Living Translation, copyright © 1996, 2004, 2007, 2013, 2015 by Tyndale House Foundation. Used by permission of Tyndale House Publishers, Inc., Carol Stream, Illinois 60188. All rights reserved.

Names: Keefer, Mikal, 1954- author. | Harrington, David, 1964- illustrator.
Title: Friends with God devotions for kids : 54 delightfully fun ways to grow closer to Jesus, family, and friends / Mikal Keefer ; illustrated by David Harrington.
Description: Loveland, CO : Group Publishing, Inc., [2017]
Identifiers: LCCN 2017029729 (print) | LCCN 2017007579 (ebook) | ISBN 9781470748623 (hardcover) | ISBN 9781470750275 (ePub)
Subjects: LCSH: Bible--Devotional literature--Juvenile literature. | Bible stories, English. | Christian children--Prayers and devotions--Juvenile literature.
Classification: LCC BS491.5 .K44 2017 (ebook) | LCC BS491.5 (print) | DDC 242/.62--dc23
LC record available at https://lccn.loc.gov/2017029729

PRINT ISBN 978-1-4707-4862-3 | EPUB ISBN 978-1-4707-5027-5
10 9 8 7 6 5 4 3 2   26 25 24 23 22 21 20 19 18 17
Printed in China.
002 China 0817

BRING YOUR DEVOTION TO LIFE WITH THE FREE FRIENDS WITH GOD APP!

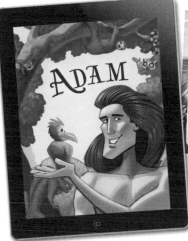

ADAM

Best known for: First human

Job: Animal namer

Hometown: Garden of Eden

Favorite food: Definitely NOT fruit

Jesus Connection: The name Adam means "man." Just like the first Adam, we all have a physical human body. And because of Jesus, we have a spiritual body, too. That's why Jesus was sometimes called the "last Adam."

Come face to face with Bible-times friends of God. Scattered throughout the pages of the *Friends With God Devotions for Kids*, digital triggers unlock mobile games so you can win virtual devotional cards with fun ideas you can talk about with your family. Plus, you'll get a Bible character collectible card with entertaining facts about that person.

Get started in three easy steps:

1. With your parents' help, download the free app available on iTunes and Google Play.

   Available on the App Store   **ANDROID APP ON Google play**

2. When you see this icon 😊, scan the page with your mobile device.

3. Play the games to win all of the collectible cards!

TABLE OF CONTENTS

HERE'S something you might not know: God likes you—a *lot*.

He likes spending time with you because that's what friends do. They hang out together. They talk. They listen.

And sometimes they giggle, too.

So here are 54 chances for you to spend time with God. You'll do all the stuff friends do: talk...listen...and get to know each other.

Sound good?

You'll meet some of God's friends who ended up in the Bible. That's a good thing because you can learn a *lot* about God by seeing how he acts around other people.

In each of these devotions you'll do a little reading, do a little drawing or writing, and then go have fun with your friends and family...and you can invite God along for that, too.

You'll love growing closer to God. And your family. And your friends!

So pick a devotion (you don't have to start at the front of the book unless you want to) and dive in.

Have fun!

GOD CREATES ADAM AND EVE

What God did in the beginning was AMAZING!

He called out, "Let there be light," and zillions of stars glittered in the heavens. He formed the earth, stretching sandy beaches between dry land and sparkling oceans. He told plants and trees to sprout, and the land blossomed.

Then God created life in the oceans. Fish flashed and jellyfish floated beneath the waves. Dolphins leapt and danced on the water.

Then God called for birds to fill the air and animals to scamper, crawl, and run across the land.

And finally God made the first man—Adam. And the first woman—Eve.

God paused to look at all he'd created, all that stretched out to the ends of the earth and beyond. He'd made each and every creation for a reason, and he smiled as he saw that it was all good—very good!

(Genesis 1 and 2)

Meanwhile, in *your* world...

When God made you, he did a great job! Draw a quick self-portrait, and list three things God did really well when he made you. That cute dimple, maybe, or your truly superior skating skills! Create your masterpiece here:

You and God...

Those wonderful touches God added when he made you? He gave them to you for a reason...maybe so you can use them to help others. Take a minute to ask God about that. Ask, "How can I use your good work in me to help other people?" and then see if he gives you some ideas. If so, jot them down here:

You and others...

Go rustle up a friend or two (family members count!) to play Build a Beat. Here's how to play: Clap out a short rhythm—two claps, a pause, and two more claps, for instance. The other players repeat what you did and add their own rhythms. Everyone repeats and then adds to create something cool for as long as you all can go. Fun with two, a hoot with three, creative chaos with five!

Friendship Nugget

Friends notice when other friends do good work. Tell God, "Hey, nice job!" ⟫⟫⟶

ADAM AND EVE HAVE A CHOICE

The garden where God placed Adam and Eve was perfect—lush and green. God told Adam and Eve to enjoy eating any fruit they found, except for one. It grew on a beautiful tree planted in the very center of the Garden of Eden.

One day, a snake hissed to Eve that God hadn't meant what he'd said. Of course it was okay to try the forbidden fruit. Eating it would make her wise, just like God.

As the snake urged her on, Eve plucked a piece of forbidden fruit and took a nibble.

When nothing happened, she handed the fruit to Adam—who shrugged and took a big, juicy bite.

Suddenly, it was as if their eyes had been pried wide open. They knew they'd chosen to do evil rather than good and then noticed something else: *they were naked!* They scrambled to cover themselves with fig leaves.

That evening they heard God strolling in the garden. God asked them, "Have you eaten the forbidden fruit?" Spoiler alert: God already knew the answer.

Adam pointed at Eve. Eve blamed the serpent for tricking her. The snake didn't say anything.

As a punishment for disobeying him, God made Adam and Eve leave the perfect garden they'd called home.

(Genesis 3)

Meanwhile, in *your* world...

Like Adam and Eve, you make choices. Tell God about a choice you're making now. Maybe you're deciding what to do about a bully or where to start on a book report that's due...tomorrow.

Whatever choice you're making, describe it here:

You and God...

Think about this: God knows what you wrote—and he cares about it. That's because, as your friend, he cares about you. Give God two thumbs-up, big time: one thumb for making time to know you while running the universe and one thumb for also caring about you!

You and others...

Find a couple of people to play Two Truths and a Lie. Take turns telling one another two true things about yourself and one lie. See if you can all choose truth from among the lies. If Adam and Eve had done that, we might all still be living in a garden!

The woman was convinced. She saw that the tree was beautiful and its fruit looked delicious, and she wanted the wisdom it would give her. So she took some of the fruit and ate it. Then she gave some to her husband, who was with her, and he ate it, too. (Genesis 3:6)

Friendship Nugget

Friends make choices that build trust in the friendship. ⇒

NOAH BUILDS AN ARK

Times were tough: Pretty much the whole world was disobeying God. Only Noah lived in a way that pleased God.

So God warned Noah a flood was coming that would scrub the earth clean and give it a do-over. Which sounded fine until Noah realized that meant everyone would drown... including him.

Uh-oh. God quickly promised that Noah and his family would be saved. But Noah had to build a boat—a *huge* boat, called an ark.

Noah got busy, and shortly after he finished the ark, rains thundered down. Geysers erupted from beneath the ground. The ark—packed tight with Noah, his family, and an entire zoo of animals—lifted and floated free.

For months they bobbed through swirling water. Then, as flood waters drained away, Noah's ark bumped to a resting spot atop a mountain. Thanks to God, Noah and his family had lived through the flood!

God told Noah to open the door of the ark and let the animals out to go find new homes. Then Noah and his family built an altar and praised God for giving the world a do-over.

(Genesis 6–9)

Meanwhile, in *your* world...

Go find a square of toilet paper and a ballpoint pen. We can wait...

You back? Good.

Now write on the toilet paper something you've said or done that you're sorry for. That you wish you could get a do-over for.

You and God...

One way to get a do-over is to apologize to the person you hurt. Ask God if that's something he'd like you to do and, if so...well, do it.

But for now, just hold the paper in your hand. Show it to God. Because when you hurt others, you're hurting him, too. Tell him you're sorry and then...

Go flush it. That's how it works when God forgives you—your sin is gone. Forgotten. Thanks to Jesus, our sins can disappear in one satisfying sin-swirly!

You and others...

Get ready to give a friend unlimited do-overs! Find a partner to play Rock, Paper, Scissors and keep playing until your friend wins three times in a row. Pack a lunch—the odds of that happening right away are like one in...um...14 zillion. Unless you're *really* bad at Rock, Paper, Scissors!

Friendship Nugget

Friends give friends do-overs. Like God's forgiven you, you can forgive others. ⋙⟶

GOD PROMISES ABRAM A SON

God came to Abram in a vision and told him, "I'll protect you, and your reward will be great."

Abram was thankful but told God what he *really* wanted was a child. What good were blessings and money without the pitter-patter of little feet in the tent? Without anyone to pass the blessings to when Abram passed away?

God nudged Abram to step outside and look up at the stars glittering overhead in the quiet night sky. "That's how many descendants you'll have," God said. And Abram believed God's promise.

God also promised that Abram's descendants would live in their own homeland. Not that their lives would be easy—God never promised *that*. In fact, God told Abram a time was coming when his descendants would become slaves.

What's a "descendant"?

You're a descendant! Your parents and grandparents are your ancestors, so you're their descendant. Your children and grandchildren will be *your* descendants.

But Abram trusted God to keep his promises, and God didn't disappoint—God did all he promised, and more!

(Genesis 15)

Meanwhile, in *your* world...

Write about a promise someone made to you that the person kept—and it mattered a lot to you. What was the promise, and who made it?

You and God...

If the person who kept that promise to you is still around, how about texting the person with a "thank you"? Remind the person that his or her actions are a reminder to you that you want to keep your promises, too. That'll be a cool text to receive.

And if God's made a promise to you that you're glad God kept, send a text God's direction, too. How? Well, that's up to you...but definitely write it!

You and others...

Gather a few friends and play a game of If I'm Elected I Promise... The goal is to get yourself elected Prime Minister of Everything by making promises of what you'll do if people vote for you.

Take turns seeing who can make the biggest whopper-promises that might swing the vote their way!

P.S. If you're elected you're gonna be in *so* much trouble...

Then the Lord took Abram outside and said to him, "Look up into the sky and count the stars if you can. That's how many descendants you will have!" (Genesis 15:5)

Friendship Nugget

If you always keep your promises to friends, you'll be the sort of friend people always want to keep. ⇒⟶

GOD PROMISES SARAH A SON

When three strangers told Abraham (the same guy who used to go by "Abram") that his wife, Sarah, would have a baby, he wasn't sure what to think.

But Sarah, sneaking a listen from inside a tent, knew *exactly* what to think: She laughed. She was old. No *way* would she give birth to a baby.

And Sarah didn't "ha-ha" laugh. She laughed the way you do when you've heard something silly—an eye-rolling, smirky, shake-your-head sort of laugh.

But a year later, Isaac was born—just like those three mysterious strangers had promised. And now Sarah was laughing a new laugh. A joyful laugh. A happy, light-up-your-face laugh that started in her eyes and ran all the way down to her toes.

Yes, she thought as she snuggled Isaac close. *God is good! God has brought me new life! God has brought me laughter!*

Laughter wrapped up in Isaac's bright giggles—whose name means "he will laugh"!

(Genesis 18 and 21)

Meanwhile, in *your* world...

Quick: List or draw five things that make you laugh. A good joke, cat playing piano videos (really?), a favorite movie, a wacky friend... whatever.

Question: How can you get more of what makes you laugh into your life?

You and God...

Think of a favorite joke—one you'd tell a parent. Got it? Now tell the joke to God. Why? Because friends like to make each other laugh, to relax, to enjoy being together. And besides, maybe God hasn't heard that one yet.

You and others...

Invite a few friends or family members to join you doing something you listed that makes you laugh. Call it a Gigglefestapalooza!

Friendship Nugget

Friends laugh *with* each other—not *at* each other. ≫————

> And Sarah declared, "God has brought me laughter. All who hear about this will laugh with me."
>
> (Genesis 21:6)

JACOB AND ESAU— TOGETHER AGAIN

Jacob and Esau were two grown-up brothers who didn't get along.

That's because, while their father was dying, Jacob pretended to be Esau. Jacob tricked his father into putting him in charge and giving him most of the family fortune.

Esau was mad. *Really* mad. So mad he wanted to *kill* Jacob. And though Jacob was a sneak, he wasn't a stupid sneak—he went to live far away with an uncle.

Years passed and Jacob became so rich that his cousins figured he must be stealing from them. They kicked Jacob out, so Jacob had no choice but to go back home...where Esau was waiting.

Esau, the brother Jacob had cheated. The brother who hated him. Yikes!

Jacob's knees were knocking when he first saw Esau. Would Esau hurt him? Fire arrows at him? Nope! Esau hugged his brother and kissed him on the cheek.

God had worked in Esau's heart to heal the hate. God helped make things right between Jacob and Esau!

(Genesis 27, 31, 32, and 33)

me

Meanwhile, in *your* world...

That's you in the middle there. Around you, draw people you're not getting along with for some reason. That bully at school, the brother or sister who's always in your face, some friend who let you down. Then draw a dotted line between you and each of those people.

You and God...

Use a finger to slowly trace the dotted line between you and each of those people you drew, one at a time. As you do, pray for the people. Ask God what you can do to help make things right between you and your dotted-line people. Listen. And then, if you're willing, do what God tells you.

You and others...

Say "I'm sorry" to someone. Hey, at least *part* of the problem with some of those dotted-line people is on you, right? So step up and apologize. It's a first step that may lead to wonderful stuff down the road.

Friendship Nugget

When you apologize, "I'm sorry" doesn't usually cut it. Say what you did that was wrong, that you're sorry, and that you won't do it again. *That's* an apology. ⟫

God's Plan for Joseph

Joseph was his father's favorite son. That made his 11 brothers (yup—11!) so angry they sold Joseph as a slave.

Which was part of God's plan for Joseph. Joseph was sold to an important Egyptian man whose wife lied about Joseph. So Joseph went to jail—and *that* was part of God's plan, too.

Because God told Joseph what dreams meant, Joseph was let out of jail to work for Pharaoh, the king of Egypt. He interpreted an important dream for the king.

Soon he was Pharaoh's go-to guy for running the country. Yup—all part of God's plan.

Back in the country where Joseph's brothers lived, the crops quit growing. People were hungry, so Joseph's brothers came to buy grain from Egypt. They didn't know the important man they met was really that skinny little brother they'd sold into slavery—and for a while Joseph didn't tell them.

Joseph finally told his brothers who he was and that he forgave them. Getting Joseph to Egypt was God's plan all along, part of a big picture even through the ups and downs. Now Joseph could save his family!

(Genesis 37–50)

Meanwhile, in *your* world...

Joseph's journey zigzagged all *over* the place: favorite son to slave to jailbird to Egyptian Big Cheese. Jot down some of the ups and downs you've had on *your* journey here:

You and God...

Joseph thanked God even for the tough times because he knew they were all part of God's plan. Try doing the same. Ask God: What can I learn from tough times that will help me better serve you and others?

You and others...

It's Family Exercise Time! Stun your family by suggesting that everyone click off their screens and join you for five minutes of jumping jacks, squats, and other up-and-down exercises. If someone can't participate for some reason, make that person a designated cheerleader.

End by thanking everyone for joining you—not just for the past five minutes but through *all* of life's ups and downs!

"Please, come closer," he said to them. So they came closer. And he said again, "I am Joseph, your brother, whom you sold into slavery in Egypt. But don't be upset, and don't be angry with yourselves for selling me to this place. It was God who sent me here ahead of you to preserve your lives."
(Genesis 45:4-5)

Friendship Nugget

Friends listen to one another when tough times come. Listening—*really* listening—helps.

MIRIAM PROTECTS MOSES

Baby Moses was in trouble!

Pharaoh, the king of Egypt, was worried there were too many Hebrew slaves in Egypt, so he ordered every new Hebrew baby boy to be killed.

Moses' mother hid her baby boy for three months, but at last she ran out of hiding places. She made a floating basket, tucked Moses in it, and sent Moses' big sister, Miriam, to hide the basket in reeds on the bank of the Nile. Then Miriam watched to see what would happen.

Pharaoh's daughter, the princess, came to the river to take a bath. She heard a baby crying, saw the basket, and looked inside. When she saw baby Moses looking back at her, her heart melted—and she decided to keep the baby for her own.

Miriam gulped hard and then bravely marched up to the princess. Miriam asked if the princess wanted a Hebrew woman to care for the baby until Moses was a little older. The princess agreed, and Miriam ran to get her mother.

The princess said she'd pay Moses' mother to raise him until he was ready to come live with the princess. Miriam and her mother praised God all the way home.

Baby Moses was saved! God had taken care of him through Miriam and his mother—and even a royal princess!

(Exodus 2)

Meanwhile, in *your* world...

God used Miriam to care for Moses. Who's God caring for through you? Who's he using to care *for* you? Jot your thoughts below:

You and God...

God usually shows up through people, not thunderbolts. How's God showing up in your life? For the next couple of days, watch for him. When you think you've caught a glimpse of him, whisper a "thank you" to let him know you noticed.

You and others...

It's the "Hey, You!" Quiz: Ask friends and family members to play a name game about animals who care for one another in groups. See if they know what to call groups of these animals: penguins (rookery), owls (parliament), porcupines (prickle), toads (knot), lions (pride), rhinos (crash), elephants (parade), geese (gaggle), bats (cauldron), and crows (murder).

Yes, you're allowed to tell them. And isn't it cool that God cares for animals—and us—through others?

Friendship Nugget

Friends risk standing up for one another. Sometimes God helps you out through your friends. ⋙━━▶

GOD RESCUES THE ISRAELITES

It took a *lot* to convince Pharaoh to let God's people leave Egypt.

There were plagues—10 of 'em—and the last was the worst. An angel passed over all the houses in Egypt and the firstborn son in each house died.

Because God warned his people to paint lambs' blood around the doors of their homes, the angel passed over their houses. But Egyptian families lost their oldest sons—including Pharaoh, who lost his oldest boy.

Pharaoh told God's people to leave Egypt. Scram! Then Pharaoh had second thoughts. He sent his army after God's people to herd them back. But God wanted what was best for his people and that was reaching a new homeland, one where they could worship him.

So at the Red Sea, God did something no one else could do. He parted the waters so his people could pass over to the far shore. Then, when the Egyptian army tried to follow, God let the walls of water crash back together, drowning the soldiers—and saving his people!

(Exodus 12 and 14)

Meanwhile, in *your* world...

God knew what was best for his people even if they weren't sure about it along the way. Kind of like getting a shot may help you feel better even though YOU HATE SHOTS AND NEVER WANT TO GET ANOTHER ONE EVER!

Write something that was good for you even though you didn't like it at the time:

You and God...

Do you trust that God wants to do what's best for you? If so, put your hands out in front of you with your palms facing up. Tell God you're ready to do what he tells you to do, to go where he tells you to go. And then listen—God may have something to say to you.

You and others...

Play a few rounds of Good, Better, Best, Yuck! with friends by taking turns naming something and seeing if others rank it as good, better, best, or yuck. For instance: soy milk. *You* may love it, but do your friends agree?

See how your rankings for TV shows, sports teams, or superheroes line up. And try to convince each other to change rankings.

> As Pharaoh approached, the people of Israel looked up and panicked when they saw the Egyptians overtaking them...But Moses told the people, "Don't be afraid. Just stand still and watch the Lord rescue you today. The Egyptians you see today will never be seen again. The Lord himself will fight for you. Just stay calm."
>
> (Exodus 14:10, 13-14)

Friendship Nugget
Friends want what's best for each other—always. ⇒⇒⇒

MOSES RECEIVES THE TEN COMMANDMENTS

God's people weren't sure how to obey God. So God gave them some rules to follow.

Sometimes people make up rules because they're bossy and just like to be in charge. That wasn't why God gave his people 10 rules—Ten Commandments. God gave his people rules because he didn't want them to get hurt.

When we follow God's plans for our lives, it's always for the best. When we disobey, that's when we can get in trouble. That's when we can hurt our friendship with God—and other people.

Here are the rules God gave his people: Put God first, don't make pretend gods, don't use God's name badly, keep the seventh day special for God, honor your parents, don't kill people, be true to your husband or wife, don't steal, don't lie, and don't wish you could have other people's stuff.

Following those rules would help God's people have a heart open to God— and help them not do things that were hurtful to themselves or others.

(Exodus 20)

Meanwhile, in *your* world...

What's a rule you can't wait to outgrow? Like having to go to bed at a certain time, or not being old enough to drive, or having to always order off the kids' menu at restaurants. Write That Rule You Love to Hate here:

Question: Why do you think someone made that rule? How might following it be helping you for now?

You and God...

Put a bandage on the inside of your wrist where you'll see it for the next day or two. When you do, pause and thank God for loving you and wanting to keep you safe.

You and others...

You'll need tinfoil, a sink, a stack of pennies, and some curious friends or family members for a game of Sink or Swim. You play by filling the sink half-full of water and making sure the drain is closed. Then make a raft by doubling up a large square of tinfoil a few times and curling up the edges. Ask how many pennies each person thinks the boat can hold before it sinks. See whose guess is closest.

Friendship Nugget

Friends keep one another safe. ≫>——

AARON AND THE GOLDEN CALF

While Moses was up on a mountain talking with God, his right-hand man, Aaron, made a *huge* mistake. Two mistakes, actually.

First, when God's people came to Aaron wanting his help making a fake god, Aaron went along with them. He collected gold earrings, melted the gold, and made a golden calf.

Aaron went along with the crowd and helped God's people worship the fake-god calf—instead of God. That was mistake number one.

God saw what was happening and told Moses to step back out of the way. God was ready to wipe out all his people, but when Moses asked him to hold off, God let the people live.

Moses scurried down the mountain. He quickly found Aaron and asked, "Why did you *do* this?" Aaron told Moses he'd tossed gold into a fire and when the gold melted, it just sort of came out as a calf. You know, by accident.

Um...I don't *think* so. Aaron lied—mistake number two.

Aaron had gone along with the crowd. But that didn't mean God quit loving him. God's love is bigger than our mistakes!

(Exodus 32)

Meanwhile, in *your* world...

Find a picture (download and print if necessary) of a group you'd love to be part of. A sports team, band, or maybe the elite Klingon Planetary Defense Unit. Tape that picture here, and jot down your reasons for wanting to be part of that group:

You and God...

The groups you join help shape you. That's why it matters who you hang out with...and why you *always* want to be joined to God. Face east (the sun popped up there this morning), and tell God you want to be with him in the morning. Face west and tell him you want to be with him at night. Ask him to help you pick which groups to join.

You and others...

It's Untangle the Pretzel time! You'll need at least five people (eight is better), so go recruit 'em. Stand in a circle, facing in. Have your friends each lift their left hand and grab someone else's hand. Then repeat with right hands. You've created a human pretzel! Have everyone carefully climb under and over each other to untangle the knot.

> They said to me, "Make us gods who will lead us. We don't know what happened to this fellow Moses, who brought us here from the land of Egypt." So I told them, "Whoever has gold jewelry, take it off." When they brought it to me, I simply threw it into the fire—and out came this calf!
>
> (Exodus 32:23-24)

Friendship Nugget

Friends don't force friends to "go along or else." They respect each other. ⟫⟶

CALEB'S COURAGE

God's people were camped on the edge of the Promised Land. They knew people lived there already, people they'd probably have to fight.

So a dozen spies crept into the land to take a look at who—and what—was there. The spies came back with good news...and bad news.

The good news: It was a wonderful place, overflowing with fruit and crops.

The bad news: It was *also* overflowing with tribes who lived in forts and knew how to fight. There were even giants wandering around.

Of all the spies, only Joshua and Caleb thought God's people could win the land. The other spies were knee-knocking afraid and ready to turn around.

Caleb knew how hard the fight might be, but he trusted God. If God was with them, what were a few giants? God is bigger than them—and our fears!

(Numbers 13)

Meanwhile, in *your* world...

Some of the spies were scared of large people living in the Promised Land. Draw the *largest* thing you're scared of below. And the *smallest* thing you're scared of!

You and God...

Notice the American penny says "In God We Trust." God's bigger than anything that might frighten you—that's true no matter how you feel. But if you want your heart rate to go down, you have to remember to *trust* God. Put a finger on this coin and tell God you trust him, and why.

You and others...

God sent out spies once and he may do it again, so you better be prepared. Make a mustache disguise for yourself and everyone else in your family (see illustration). When your whole family (except for the dog...and goldfish) is mustached–up, talk about this: If you were a super-spy, how would you use your spy powers?

Friendship Nugget

Friends don't make fun of us when we're afraid. They help us be brave like God helps us be brave. ⫸

BALAAM'S TALKING DONKEY

It was an interesting day for the donkey.

His owner, Balaam, was busy ignoring what God wanted as Balaam rode the donkey to a meeting. So God sent an angel to block the donkey's way.

Three times the donkey—who could see the angel—paused in the road. And three times Balaam—who *couldn't* see the angel—whipped the donkey to get him to keep moving forward. Finally, to get Balaam's attention, God let the donkey talk.

"You've been riding me your whole life," the donkey said. "Have I ever done anything like this before?"

Balaam had to admit the donkey hadn't ever disobeyed. Or talked, for that matter.

Then God opened Balaam's eyes to see the angel. A large angel. A large angel with a sword, ready to kill one very disobedient Balaam had his donkey carried Balaam any closer to the angel.

Balaam slid off the donkey and fell facedown on the ground.

Now God had Balaam's attention!

(Numbers 22)

Meanwhile, in *your* world...

What's the best way for God to get your attention? A talking donkey? A letter? A text? Jot down the ways you think God should use to make sure you're listening:

You and God...

God used lots of ways to get people's attention—just ask Balaam. But mostly God wants us to just listen to him. Practice by sitting quietly and noticing everything you hear—people talking, a TV in the other room. Then ask God to speak to you, and listen for him as well.

Write down anything you hear or feel here:

You and others...

Have a Mumble Conversation with a friend or family member. It's like a regular conversation; but each of you has to talk through clenched teeth without moving your lips. And NO LAUGHING! See how long you can go before moving a lip or letting go with a giggle. Good luck!

> Then the Lord opened Balaam's eyes, and he saw the angel of the Lord standing in the roadway with a drawn sword in his hand. Balaam bowed his head and fell face down on the ground before him.
>
> (Numbers 22:31)

Friendship Nugget

Friends give each other the chance to explain. ➤➤➤

Rahab Protects Two Spies

When two of Israel's spies crossed the Jordan River and passed through the city gates of Jericho, they were walking into a trap.

They thought nobody knew them. That they could check out the city walls and then slide back out the same way they'd walked in.

But someone knew they were there—and told the king of Jericho. The city gates slammed shut. Jericho was locked down, soldiers going house to house to find the spies.

The spies hiding in Rahab's house.

Rahab had an *awful* reputation—nobody would expect her to help trapped spies. But Rahab not only hid them on the roof of her house, she also told soldiers who banged on her door that the spies weren't there.

And then she helped the spies find a way out of Jericho.

Rahab was an unlikely person for God to use to help the spies—but that's what God did. God works through *lots* of unlikely people. He did it in Rahab's time, and he's still doing it today.

(Joshua 2)

Meanwhile, in *your* world...

Who's someone you may not even like who's still helping you? That teacher...a coach who yells at you all the time...a bad-attitude big brother. Think of two or three, and in the space below write their names and how God is working through them. For instance, maybe that YELLING ALL THE TIME coach is helping you get in better shape.

You and God...

Those names on your list? Those are people to thank God for. Hold your list up to a lightbulb to discover what you can see from the next page shining through the names you wrote.

Ask God to help you see him working through the people on your list...and to be grateful for them.

You and others...

Up for a game of Hide and Seek? Decide on boundaries (just in the house, or somewhere outside) and have at it. Extra points for catching everyone...and no leaving people hiding behind the sofa and going out for pizza without telling them!

Friendship Nugget

Friends appreciate what people do for them. Have you thanked God lately for what he's doing for you? ⋙

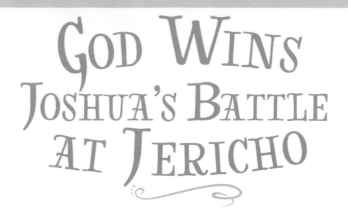

GOD WINS
JOSHUA'S BATTLE AT JERICHO

Fighting a battle is scary. You might get hurt. You could lose.

But when God's fighting for you...well, it's easy to have courage!

When God's people needed to take the walled city of Jericho, they had a problem. They'd have to fight their way *to* the walls and then find a way *over* the walls—all while Jericho's army was shooting arrows down on them. Ouch!

But God had a better plan: Silently march around the city once a day for six days.

Then, on the seventh day, march, blow one long horn blast, and scream as loud as you can. Do that, God said, and Jericho's walls will fall down.

"Have courage," God told the army's general, Joshua. "I've got this for you."

Joshua did as God told him and sure enough: Joshua watched Jericho's walls crumble! And God's people won the battle!

(Joshua 6)

Meanwhile, in *your* world...

Sometimes God asks us to do stuff that just doesn't make sense...at first. Love your enemies. Forgive someone more than once. Give some of your money away. March around walls and then blow a horn.

What's something you know God wants you to do that sort of doesn't make sense to you? Draw a picture of you doing it here:

And here's a question for you: Has God given you the courage to do it anyway?

You and God...

The only way Jericho's walls were coming down was if God *knocked* them down—so he did. What's something big and nasty you're facing that you can't knock down on your own? As you walk in a circle around your room, tell God about it.

You and others...

It takes courage to trust others like Joshua trusted God. See for yourself with a game of Tipper. Pair up with someone about your same height. Decide who's the Tipper and who's the Catcher. The Catcher will stand right behind the Tipper.

Then the Tipper will raise his arms slightly, lock his legs, and tip backward. The Catcher will be ready to tuck his arms under the arms of the Tipper, breaking the Tipper's fall. Take turns tipping and catching. Practice having courage!

Friendship Nugget

Friends trust one another and help one another trust God.

> Now the gates of Jericho were tightly shut because the people were afraid of the Israelites. No one was allowed to go out or in. But the Lord said to Joshua, "I have given you Jericho, its king, and all its strong warriors."
>
> (Joshua 6:1-2)

Deborah Helps Barak

For 20 years the Canaanites made life hard for God's people. The Canaanites had a strong army, so they came whenever they wanted and took whatever they wanted—and they wanted a *lot*.

At that time a woman named Deborah was a judge for God's people. She sat out under a palm tree where people could find her, and when Israelites had a problem, they came to her for advice. Everyone knew: Deborah was wise.

But she was also a woman, and in her time, women didn't give advice about how to win wars. That was something men were supposed to do.

Except God gave Deborah wisdom. God told her how Israel could beat the Canaanite army. Because Deborah was wise, she listened and then told Barak, an Israelite leader, about God's plan.

And because Barak was *also* wise, he listened to Deborah and followed God's plan.

All of which led to a very bad day for the Canaanites. When their army came roaring into battle, God caused them to become confused—and Barak's soldiers took it from there. They chased their enemies until the entire Canaanite army was destroyed.

(Judges 4)

Meanwhile, in *your* world...

If God gave you wisdom, what problems would you like to solve? World peace? A family thing? Draw a picture here that answers that question:

You and God...

God gives wisdom—to you and others, too, if he's asked. And nobody needs more wisdom than leaders.

List some of the leaders you know who need God's help making good decisions. Leaders in your family, church, school, town, and country. As you write your list, ask God to give each person a Deborah-sized dose of wisdom!

You and others...

Part of wisdom is learning from experience. Ask a few friends or family members to cover one eye with a hand and, with the other hand, toss a crumpled piece of paper at a target—a paper cup, maybe. With one eye covered, your ~~victims~~ friends will find it hard to aim because they've lost depth perception. See if their aim gets better with practice— that's what wisdom is like!

Friendship Nugget

Friends think before they give advice to one another.

GIDEON'S BATTLE

Gideon was *not* the guy you'd pick to lead an army. He was from a weak clan. He wasn't even the strongest guy in his family.

Still, God picked him to lead an attack on the Midianites, who'd stormed into Israel and were starving God's people. God saw something in Gideon that others didn't see. Not even Gideon saw it.

God saw the best in Gideon...that Gideon would obey and rely on God.

When Gideon put together his army, God told him it was too big. *Huh*? But Gideon trusted God, so he sent thousands of men home.

When God thought there were *still* too many soldiers, Gideon got his army of 30,000 men down to just 300 men.

Three. Hundred. Men. Not enough—but Gideon relied on God.

Gideon gave each man a ram's horn, clay jar, and a torch. Late at night, Gideon's mini-army crept up to the edge of the Midianite camp, surrounding it. Then, at Gideon's signal, the 300 men blew their horns and held high torches they'd hidden in their jars.

The Midianite soldiers were so scared they began fighting *one another* in the darkness!

God saw in Gideon what he looks for in everyone: a heart willing to hear and obey, and a desire to rely on God in every situation. That's the best in us!

(Judges 6 and 7)

Meanwhile, in *your* world...

God sees the best in you even if you don't see it yourself. You probably pay more attention to the things you wish you could change, but God focuses on the good stuff he built into you. Draw yourself below the way God sees you:

You and God...

Get a cup of water and slowly empty it into a sink. As you do, ask God to help you empty out thoughts about how you're not good enough and to instead fill you with thoughts about how you can use what he's given you to serve him and others. Then fill the glass again and take a long drink of cool, refreshing, life-giving water. Ahhh!

You and others...

Find some family or friends, pens, and paper and draw No-Peeking Portraits. Look carefully at someone and then, with your eyes closed, draw a portrait—making sure to especially highlight the finer features. NOTE: You'll probably send your pen skidding off the paper, so sketch on something you don't mind getting marked up!

> Then the Lord turned to him and said, "Go with the strength you have, and rescue Israel from the Midianites. I am sending you!" "But Lord," Gideon replied, "how can I rescue Israel? My clan is the weakest in the whole tribe of Manasseh, and I am the least in my entire family!"
>
> (Judges 6:14-15)

Friendship Nugget

Friends see the best in each other—because they *look* for it!

Ruth, Naomi, and a Lasting Friendship

When Ruth married Naomi's son, the two women became relatives. But then something cool happened: They also became *friends*.

And, like lots of friends do, when hard times came they helped each other. That was true when Naomi's husband died and also true when her son, Ruth's husband, died.

That left Naomi and Ruth with no husbands to support them. Naomi told Ruth to go back home—her family lived nearby—so she could stay with relatives until she married again.

As for Naomi, she was going back to Bethlehem where she had family.

Ruth wouldn't abandon her dear friend Naomi. Even though moving to Bethlehem meant Ruth would leave everything she was used to behind, she promised to stick with Naomi.

God had given them their friendship, and friends stand by one another.

The walk to Bethlehem was a long, hard hike. But once they got there, the two women found the help they needed. Ruth met Boaz, a kind man who let her gather grain from his fields...and Ruth later married him.

Ruth had made good on her promise to go where Naomi went, to let Naomi's people become her people.

The women remained friends for the rest of their lives.

(Ruth 1 and 2)

Meanwhile, in *your* world...

Write what you like most about your friends. Maybe it's their sense of humor or that they're kind. Or that they give you their used bubble gum to chew. Okay, probably not that last one. But whatever you like—list it here:

Extra points for *telling* your friends why you like them!

You and God...

Ruth and Naomi were besties for *real*. Pull up a list of your friends' names on your cellphone and pray for those friends. (No phone? No problem! Write down the names instead.) Ask God to be with them and draw them closer to him.

You and others...

It's time for a feisty game of Friend Juggling!
Get a few friends in a circle and each of you
pull off one shoe. You play like this: On the
count of three, you each *gently* toss a shoe to
another person...and it can be anyone. So, like,
Braxton could get no
shoes tossed his way,
or 17. Big fun...unless
you're Braxton. Make
this cooler by tossing a
compliment along with
the shoe!

> But Ruth replied, "Don't
> ask me to leave you and
> turn back. Wherever you
> go, I will go; wherever you
> live, I will live. Your people
> will be my people, and
> your God will be my God."
> (Ruth 1:16)

Friendship Nugget

Friends tell each other what
they like about
one another.

HANNAH'S PRAYER
for
A SON

Hannah was heartbroken.

She wanted a son, but she and her husband hadn't been able to have a baby.

So Hannah walked slowly to the Tabernacle, pausing outside the entrance. Choking back sobs she closed her eyes and poured her heart out to God. Hannah didn't trust her voice so she only mouthed her prayer, her lips moving silently as tears slid down her cheeks.

And that's when Eli, the priest sitting near the Tabernacle's entrance, interrupted her.

"You're drunk," Eli scolded, wagging a critical finger at her.

But Eli was wrong. He'd only seen a weeping woman. He hadn't heard her prayers.

God heard Hannah's prayers, though. God heard Hannah beg for a son and promise that, if God gave her one, she'd give the boy back to God.

A year later Hannah held her son, Samuel, in her arms. God had given her the deepest desire of her heart.

(1 Samuel 1)

Meanwhile, in *your* world...

Draw your family tree here. Aren't sure who's on it? Get some help from an older family member!

You and God...

GOD IS LISTENING SO YOU DON'T HAVE TO SHOUT...but why not try? Find a spot where you think you'll hear an echo (spoiler alert: bathrooms usually work), and shout out a quick prayer. God hears you even when you whisper, but when's the last time you gave God a shout-out? But, umm...don't do this in a *public* bathroom—that just scares people.

You and others...

Gather your family together and then read the following statements, asking your family to help fill in the blanks. The only rule: Everything said has to be positive as you build one another up.

- I remember when [family member] did a great job on _____.

- I remember when we [something fun you did together].

- I remember when [family member] helped me by doing _____.

Friendship Nugget

Friends share memories together. ≫———▶

Samuel Picks a King

Samuel had no idea what to do. None.

God told him to pick one of Jesse's sons to be the next king of Israel. But Jesse had *eight* sons—which one was Samuel supposed to pick?

Samuel took a look at each young man, one at a time. He thought the oldest son looked kingly: tall and handsome. But God warned Samuel to not judge based on looks. *People* judge based on looks, but *God* pays more attention to the heart.

So Samuel met Jesse's sons, one after another, and none of them was the king God had in mind for his people. Uh-oh. What was Samuel missing?

Samuel scratched his head and asked if Jesse had any other sons hanging around the farm—any sons he hadn't already seen.

"Well," Jesse said, "There's my youngest boy, David. He's out in the fields guarding sheep and goats." Jesse hadn't thought Samuel would even consider David for the job.

"Bring him in," Samuel said. "Let's take a look."

When David walked in the room, God told Samuel that *this* young man was the one. *This* was the next king. God had looked past David's young age to see his heart—and God saw the heart of a king.

(1 Samuel 16)

Meanwhile, in *your* world...

Write about a time you changed your mind about someone. Who was it—and why did you change your mind?

Hmmm... What might you learn from what you wrote?

You and God...

Borrow another person's prescription glasses and put them on. Look around—whoaaah! It's a different way to see the world, huh? Close your eyes and ask God to help you see the world the way *he* sees it...and people the way *he* sees them. Then take off those glasses and return them before you get a headache!

You and others...

Sometimes things (and people!) aren't what they seem at first—like a Flubber Pencil. With friends take turns doing this easy trick: Using your thumb and forefinger, hold a yellow pencil by the eraser. Bounce the pencil up and down—it'll look like it's made out of rubber.

Hey, why not try some other stuff around the house to see what else works for this trick, too?

> But the Lord said to Samuel, "Don't judge by his appearance or height, for I have rejected him. The Lord doesn't see things the way you see them. People judge by outward appearance, but the Lord looks at the heart."
>
> (1 Samuel 16:7)

Friendship Nugget

Friends like God take the time to really get to know you. >>>

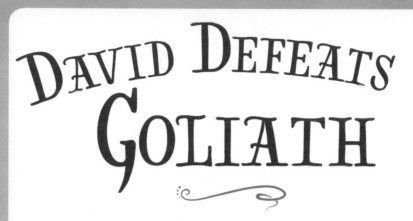

DAVID DEFEATS GOLIATH

Nobody was betting on David in the Great David/Goliath Showdown.

First, because Goliath was a Philistine giant, nine feet of solid muscle and bad attitude. David was...David. Nice kid, but no match for a seasoned soldier like Goliath.

And second? Well, see reason number one.

When David reached the front lines of Israel's war with the Philistines, he discovered there was no fighting. Goliath had been challenging any Israelite to fight him, and there were no takers.

So carrying just the sling he used to kill wild animals and a couple of rocks, David walked boldly out to do battle.

David knew something Goliath didn't: *God was on his side*. That meant Goliath didn't stand a chance.

The fight was over after just one shot!

When David's stone missile smashed into Goliath's forehead, the giant toppled onto the dusty field. THUNK!

For a long moment, nobody in either army moved. Or breathed.

Then one Philistine soldier...and then another...and then an entire Philistine army turned tail and ran for their lives.

(1 Samuel 17)

Meanwhile, in *your* world...

Draw a picture of your Goliath. Maybe it's a person...maybe an illness...maybe a problem you're facing at home.

Draw it, and then ask God to be with you as you face it. God is on your side!

You and God...

David knew he'd be okay because God was on his side. But even if Goliath had picked David up and torn him in two, David was *still* okay. Dead or alive, David was with God. And if you know Jesus, you get to be with God always! That's worth celebrating!

Celebrate however you best celebrate (jump, twirl, applaud...) as you thank God for always being on your side and by your side!

You and others...

Target practice! Crumple up some paper wads and launch them at the paper cup you've balanced on the head of the tallest person in the room. If you happen to have a friend who plays professional basketball, this is the time to invite him over!

> David replied to the Philistine, "You come to me with sword, spear, and javelin, but I come to you in the name of the Lord of Heaven's Armies—the God of the armies of Israel, whom you have defied. Today the Lord will conquer you...and the whole world will know that there is a God in Israel!"
>
> (1 Samuel 17:45-46)

Friendship Nugget

Friends show up when they're needed. ⟫⟫⟫▬

ABIGAIL MAKES PEACE

Abigail groaned when she heard the news.

Her husband, Nabal, had refused when messengers from David's army asked for food. Even worse, Nabal had made fun of David's men and then chased them away. How rude! And after David's men had helped keep Nabal's flocks safe!

Which meant David would soon be back—to get even.

Abigail snapped into action. As David and 400 soldiers neared her home, they met Abigail on the road—and she'd brought mountains of food with her.

Abigail slipped off her donkey and knelt before David. She apologized, asking David to not settle the score by killing her husband and workers. Nabal had been wrong to not honor David's past kindness, and she wanted to make things right. God could help them all get along with each other.

That's when David realized what he'd been about to do. Was he really going to murder Nabal and his guards because of an insult? Yes—until Abigail had caused David to pause...calm down...and see that she was right: God *could* help them get along.

(1 Samuel 25)

Meanwhile, in *your* world...

Who's a friend you want to get along with, someone who really matters to you? Cut the letters of that person's name out of a magazine or paper, and glue them below.

You and God...

Getting along with friends takes talking with them. About big stuff. Small stuff. All *kinds* of stuff. That's true for all your friendships—including your friendship with God.

Find a quiet spot and have a talk with God now. Tell God about something fun that happened today and something that was hard. And do this: Ask God how his day has gone. See what you hear!

You and others...

Getting along sometimes takes teamwork. Practice by finding someone and doing this: Place a penny on a tabletop and, working together with each of you using just one index finger, pick up the penny and put it in a cup.

Friendship Nugget

Real friends are willing to forgive one another.

SOLOMON'S WISDOM

Solomon could have asked for anything: money...a long life...to be fabulously famous and live on the beach.

But when God asked Solomon—who'd just become king of Israel—what Solomon wanted, the new king said, "I want wisdom so I can rule well and be a good king."

God *loved* that answer and gave Solomon the wisdom the new king wanted.

Wisdom is having good judgment, making good decisions. It's knowing how to do the right thing even when it's not clear what the right thing is.

Like when two women came to Solomon, both claiming to be the mother of a baby. Both women said the same thing: "That kid is *mine*, and that woman is lying!"

Solomon listened and then asked for a sword. Just cut the kid in half and give each woman half a baby—that would solve things.

One of the women quickly screamed, "No! Don't kill the baby! Give him to her so the baby can live!" The other woman just shrugged. Sure, cut the baby in half. Why not?

Solomon gave the baby to the woman who'd rushed to give up the child rather than see it harmed. If she loved the baby that much, she must be the real mother.

That's wisdom. And that's what God was willing to give Solomon.

(1 Kings 3; Proverbs 1 and 2)

Meanwhile, in *your* world...

One way you can learn to make great decisions (that's part of what it means to be wise) is learning from times you make...um...*less* than great decisions.

So do this: Write about a mistake you made and what you learned from it. Maybe you tried to jump your bike off a curb. Or you decided not to tell the truth. Or you hung around with kids who told you it was okay to steal from stores. What's your mistake, and what did you learn? Write about it here:

See? You're wiser already!

You and God...

Put a pinch of salt on your tongue. You'll be thirsty for water, but even more than water you need wisdom. So ask God for it...and then go get some water!

You and others...

Part of wisdom is knowing who to trust. With a few family or friends, do a Trust Walk together.

Find a partner who'll close his or her eyes tightly. Then the sighted partner will direct the person who can't see through the house—or outdoors!

That night the Lord appeared to Solomon in a dream, and God said, "What do you want? Ask, and I will give it to you!"

"Give me an understanding heart so that I can govern your people well and know the difference between right and wrong. For who by himself is able to govern this great people of yours?"

The Lord was pleased that Solomon had asked for wisdom.

(1 Kings 3:5, 9-10)

Friendship Nugget

Friends help friends make good, life-giving choices. ⫸⟶

GOD PROVES HE'S REAL

The people of Israel had given up on God. They were worshipping Baal—a statue of a false god. But a few of God's people—including the prophet Elijah—still believed in the one true God.

So Elijah suggested a showdown on Mount Carmel. The priests of Baal—450 of them—would cut open a bull and pile the pieces on a wood-stacked stone altar. If Baal somehow lit the fire, he was real.

Elijah would do the same and see if God showed up with a match. And the people of Israel could watch to see who was real: Baal or God.

The priests of Baal went first. Hour after hour they begged Baal to show up. They prayed. They screamed and danced. They cut themselves. And nothing happened.

Elijah went next. And to make things interesting, not only did he pour water on the altar, he also dug a trench around the altar and filled *that* with water.

Then Elijah asked God—just once—to show up and prove that God was real.

In a split second a lightning bolt sizzled downward, nearly blowing the top off Mount Carmel. The bull vaporized. The wet wood—even the stones of the altar—exploded in a burst of blinding light and deafening thunder.

There was no longer *any* doubt: God was real!

(1 Kings 18)

Meanwhile, in *your* world...

Write a list of stuff you used to think was real—but now that you're older you know better. Stuff like the Easter Bunny (um...you knew he's not real, right?), and fairies, and monsters under your bed. Write your list here:

You and God...

God is real even if you don't see him. Or believe in him. He's like gravity in that way—he's there whether or not you believe.

Do this: Go to a window and place one hand on it. Ask God to help you see him clearly—to notice him working in the world...and you.

You and others...

God's a *great* shot—he fried the altar in one try! Let's see what sort of aim you and your friends have. Set a trash can at least 10 feet away. Then, one at a time, flip or toss playing cards at the can to see how many you can get inside. You get 52 tries!

Immediately the fire of the Lord flashed down from heaven and burned up the young bull, the wood, the stones, and the dust. It even licked up all the water in the trench! And when all the people saw it, they fell face down on the ground and cried out, "The Lord—he is God! Yes, the Lord is God!"

(1 Kings 18:38-39)

Friendship Nugget

Decide to be a *real* friend—to your family, friends, and God!

Elisha's Bottomless Oil Flask

The prophet Elisha had followed after Elijah, and he, too, was a faithful follower of God in the land of Israel. Among the other believers was a group of prophets who helped Elisha—and, sadly, one of them had died.

The widow of the passed-away prophet came to Elisha with a problem. Her husband had left her with debts and two sons. One of the men she owed money to was threatening to take her two sons as slaves to settle the debt.

And there was nothing she could do.

Elisha asked her to gather up as many empty jars as she could find. She scrounged up a lot of jars and then did something that made no sense: At Elisha's request she took a small flask of olive oil and began pouring it into a large jar.

The oil kept flowing and filled the jar. And the next jar. And every jar she could borrow from her neighbors.

"Now go sell the olive oil and pay off what you owe," Elisha said. "You and your sons can then live on the money left over from the sale."

God had provided exactly what the widow and her sons needed!

(2 Kings 4)

Meanwhile, in *your* world...

There's stuff you want and stuff you need. Here's one way to tell the difference: Hold your breath as you write a wish list for stuff you want in the space below. List anything—*but don't breathe* until you really, really have to.

Whew! You *want* lots of new techie stuff...but you *need* air. Quite a difference, huh?

You and God...

You know when you were trying to live without breathing air? Well, you can't do that...at least not for long.

Thank God for giving you life by thinking about your breathing for a bit. For the next couple of minutes, when you breathe in, think, *God, thank you for life*. And when you breathe out, think, *God, I praise you for your good gift*.

You and others...

Rustle up some friends or family to play Desert Island. Give people each a chance to say what they'd take with them to a deserted desert island. Food and water is already there, plus a tent. See who'd bring what, and then see if you can all agree on three things to take. Have fun! By the way, if someone says "fork," he probably thinks it's a *dessert* island made out of chocolate cake...

Friendship Nugget

When a friend needs something, you show up to help as best you can.

Josiah Discovers Scripture

Josiah had been king of Israel for 18 years when a workman, kicking around in a dusty back room at the Temple, found an old, forgotten scroll.

A scroll he rushed straight to the king.

They'd found the "Law of the Lord," something any king of Israel should know about. So Josiah's royal court secretary read it aloud— and Josiah came *unglued*.

He tore at his clothes. He wailed. He sobbed. Josiah said, "We should have been doing what's written here all along—our *ancestors* should have been doing it! They didn't...we haven't...and God must be mad!"

Josiah was right—God *was* angry.

God's people had been ignoring and disobeying him for years! But because Josiah took God's Word to heart, because Israel's king let God's Word change him, God put off punishing his people for straying far away from him.

(2 Kings 22)

Meanwhile, in *your* world...

Josiah took God seriously! Draw a picture of something you've done that someone looking might see and say, "Hey—that kid takes God seriously!"

You and God...

Josiah was changed by the words God caused to be written in a book. That can be true for you as you read the Bible, too. Sometimes God changes people by speaking words to them. Let's see if he has a word for you. Ask God what he might want you to write below:

If you wrote something, show a parent or Christian friend and talk about it.

You and others...

Here's a game you can play with just one other person: Back Page. You play this way: Using your index finger, slowly "write" letters on the person's back. See if the person can figure out what you're writing. Take turns. CAUTION: This is *not* the time to spell out G-E-T-O-U-T-N-O-W-T-H-E-R-E-I-S-A-F-I-R-E.

Friendship Nugget

When friends hang out together, they change each other—for the good.

REBUILDING THE TEMPLE

When the king of Persia gave Israelites living in Persia his okay to go back home and rebuild the Temple, they didn't waste any time. They hiked to Jerusalem just as fast as they could...and they got busy.

Soon they had a new foundation built on the old Temple foundation. True, the new Temple wouldn't be as beautiful as what Solomon had built (and the Babylonians had torn down), but it was a Temple.

And in it, they could worship God.

More than anything, God's people wanted to make a space where God could live. Where God could be praised. Where God was honored and obeyed.

And more than anything, God wanted to rebuild his people. To have a friendship with them. To see them be faithful and obedient. To know they loved him with all their hearts.

(Ezra 1, 3, and 6)

Meanwhile, in *your* world...

Draw a self-portrait. Use a pencil, crayon, or pen and draw it below. It'll all make sense in a couple of minutes when you go on reading. For now: Go all Michelangelo and sketch a masterpiece!

You and God...

God doesn't need to live in a temple anymore—he lives in people. When you know Jesus, he lives in *you*. When you were drawing yourself, you were drawing a temple.

Cool, huh? Touch your drawing (carefully, if the ink is wet) and thank God for living in you. For his Holy Spirit turning you into a temple.

For restoring you!

You and others...

God's people did some building—and you and your family or friends will, too. Except *you'll* use a deck of cards to build as tall a tower as you can in four minutes and 14 seconds. Fire up a stopwatch function on someone's phone and get crackin'!

Oh, two things: You can't cut, tear, tape, lick, stick, or fold the cards. And if you experience a tower tumble, it's okay to start over. Ready—set—build!

> The Temple of God was then dedicated with great joy by the people of Israel, the priests, the Levites, and the rest of the people who had returned from exile.
> (Ezra 6:16)

Friendship Nugget

Friends help each other become friends with God. ⋙⟶

NEHEMIAH'S WALL AROUND JERUSALEM

Nehemiah thought he had it all figured out.

The wall around Jerusalem was in awful shape. Huge holes and broken gates let sheep wander in and out of the city, so no *way* could the wall stop enemy soldiers. Something had to be done, and Nehemiah knew *he* was the guy to do it.

Nehemiah got his boss, the king of Persia, to donate building supplies. He drew up plans for fixing what had fallen down. He knew God was all for the project.

But then Nehemiah heard that people living near Jerusalem were against the wall being rebuilt. They feared the Jews becoming too powerful and having a fortress. There was angry talk about attacking Jerusalem.

So Nehemiah turned to the people—and to God.

He asked groups of people living in Jerusalem to each work on one section of the wall. He asked God to give his people the strength to get the job done.

The wall was up in just 52 days—which was, like, a world record! Jerusalem was safe again! God had shown that he was stronger than anyone who might stand against him... or his people, as they did what God wanted them to do!

(Nehemiah 2–4 and 6)

Meanwhile, in *your* world...

Who's standing against you? You know, who seems to enjoy making life hard for you? Who makes fun of you or bullies you?

Write the name of a person or two who's standing against you below:

You and God...

If there's a bully in your world, it's time to do something about it. You're going to *pray for that bully*. That's right: pray *for* him—or her. Ask God (who's stronger than any bully) to soften the bully's heart. To help the bully find joy and peace.

If you're being hurt by a bully—at school, in the neighborhood, at home, wherever—it's okay to tell a trusted adult. But remember to pray for that bully, too. God is stronger than those who are against you!

You and others...

Let's play Stackable Stuff. You can't build a wall without something to pile up, so look around—what's in the room with you? See how tall a wall you can build using what's around you.

CAUTION: Don't use anything that might get scratched. Or break. Or that's breathing. Then take some selfies of you and your wall!

> So on October 2 the wall was finished—just fifty-two days after we had begun. When our enemies and the surrounding nations heard about it, they were frightened and humiliated. They realized this work had been done with the help of our God. (Nehemiah 6:15-16)

Friendship Nugget

Friends help each other get stuff done.

QUEEN ESTHER SAVES The JEWS

When the Persian king, Xerxes, went looking for a beautiful bride, it didn't take him long to find Esther. She wasn't just pretty, she was smart. And kind. And something else the king didn't know: Esther was a Jew, one of God's chosen people.

Which wasn't a problem until the king was tricked into signing a law that every Jew in Persia was to be killed.

When Esther found out about the new law, she had to decide: Would she tell the king she was a Jew and maybe die, or hide who she was?

Esther's uncle told her that maybe God put her close to the king so she could save her people. Even though it was dangerous, God had her exactly where she needed to be.

Esther took a deep breath, marched to the throne room, and told the king...and he changed the law. Whew! God used Esther to save her people!

(Esther 5 and 8)

Meanwhile, in *your* world...

You've got a circle of friends. Some you know well, some you hardly know at all. On this set of circles, you're in the middle. Put the names of your closest friends in the circle closest to you, sorta-friends in the next circle, kinda-sorta-friends in the next circle. You get the idea.

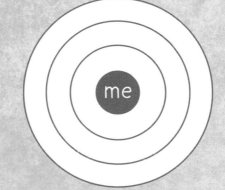

You and God...

God put you in your circle of friends for a reason. So how might God use you to help your friends become closer friends of God, too? As you look at the names you wrote, ask God how he might use you to help your friends become better friends of God.

You and others...

It's Instant Sculpture time! You're going to put people in their place—for real!

Ask friends or family members to stand and then, one at a time, turn them into human sculptures by posing them. Their job is to freeze in place. Your job is to make your mom look like *The Thinker*, and your little sister smile like the *Mona Lisa*. But be nice—they'll get a chance to pose you, too. And, yes, this is most *definitely* a pull-out-the-phone-and-take-pictures moment.

Friendship Nugget

Friends tell each other the important stuff. ➤➤➤

GOD'S PLAN FOR JOB

Job was having a bad day. A very bad day.
A very, *very* bad day.

When Satan asked God to show him a
faithful person, God pointed at Job. "He's
blameless," said God. "He steers clear of evil.
That's a faithful guy."

"Only because he's rich," Satan sniffed. "Take
away his wealth and he'll turn on
you just like everyone else."

God gave Satan permission
to test Job...and it was one
tough test!

Job lost his money. His children died. He broke out in painful sores. His grieving wife told him to curse God and die. And when three friends stopped by to cheer him up, they said pretty much the same thing.

Job finally asked God what he'd done to deserve so much trouble and pain. It wasn't fair! Why wouldn't God take away his sadness?

God reminded Job that Job couldn't understand all that God did and allowed. Job would have to trust God—and trust God's friendship.

Job listened...and agreed. And in the end, God *did* take away Job's sadness, giving back to Job much more than Job had ever lost.

(Job 1, 2, 13, 40, and 42)

Meanwhile, in *your* world...

Sometimes you lose things you *don't* get back. A person or favorite pet dies. Your parents divorce and you lose what it was like when you all lived together. You're sad...and you're not sure what to do about it.

Whatever it is, write about what you're sad that you've lost:

Now ask God to read what you've written. And to help you trust him even though you're sad.

You and God...

Using a newspaper or getting online, look at the headlines in today's news. Almost always it's bad news—news about events that made someone sad. One at a time, pray about the people behind those headlines. Ask God to be with them in their sadness, and to help them find joy in him.

You and others...

When's the last time you played Turn Those Frowns Upside Down? Not lately? Let's fix that! Recruit some friends (or nimble family members) to frown their saddest frowns and then find a way to turn those frowns upside down by turning *themselves* upside down by doing a handstand...sitting upside down on a chair...whatever works!

Friendship Nugget

Friends show up when their friends are sad. But they don't say dumb stuff to their sad friends (Job's friends = saying dumb stuff). ⟫⟫⟫

> Job stood up and tore his robe in grief. Then he shaved his head and fell to the ground to worship. He said, "I came naked from my mother's womb, and I will be naked when I leave. The Lord gave me what I had, and the Lord has taken it away. Praise the name of the Lord!" In all of this, Job did not sin by blaming God.
>
> (Job 1:20-22)

DAVID'S SHEPHERD

Two things David knew inside out: tending sheep and God.

He loved them both, and that helped David see how God was an even better friend to David than David was to his flock of sheep.

Like a good shepherd, God helped David find safety in God's love. God walked with David during hard times. And because God was with him, David didn't fear dark days.

He knew that God was watching over him—always.

God protected David and—sometimes—corrected David along the way. God poured out blessing after blessing on David.

Even when David wandered away, he trusted that God's goodness and unfailing love would come looking for him. He knew God watched over him—always.

And because David knew God's heart, David knew the best was yet to come. He wouldn't just have God for a friend in this life. He would live with God forever!

(Psalm 23)

Meanwhile, in *your* world...

Art challenge: Draw a sheep with your face on it. Then, next to the sheep, list some ways God's a good shepherd to you.

You and God...

David often wrote about how he felt knowing God was his shepherd. He liked having God always watching, always nearby. How do you feel about that? When you think about God being your shepherd, how's that feel? Write about it here:

You and others...

Did you know lots of the psalms were written to be sung? Yep—and you're bringing back the tradition with the Psuper Psalm Psingfest! See how many musical styles you can use to sing: "The Lord is my shepherd, I shall not want." Try opera, heavy metal, country, rock, gospel, hip-hop...your choice.

Extra points for accompanying yourself on air guitar. Invite friends and family to both attend and try singing. Even better: Sell tickets! It's karaoke night at your house!

> Even when I walk through the darkest valley, I will not be afraid, for you are close beside me. Your rod and your staff protect and comfort me.
> (Psalm 23:4)

Friendship Nugget

Friends watch out for each other. Which makes God a *great* friend! ⟫⟫⟫━━▶

GOD CHOOSES JEREMIAH

Jeremiah thought he wasn't ready to be a prophet.

"I'm too young!" he sputtered when God told Jeremiah he'd been chosen to speak God's words to others.

But God didn't agree. "Before you were even born I picked you for this job," God said. "And you don't have to be afraid. I'll be with you."

God knew who Jeremiah really was inside!

Was Jeremiah scared? You bet he was! Prophets sometimes found themselves standing in front of kings, pointing fingers and telling those kings they'd done wrong. That they were sinners.

Being a prophet was a wonderful way to get chased out of town...beaten to a pulp...or even worse.

God spoke gently to his friend Jeremiah. God *knew* Jeremiah—knew everything *about* Jeremiah. And God knew that, with God's help, Jeremiah could do what prophets need to do.

"So get up and get ready for action," God said as Jeremiah took a deep breath. "Tell them everything I tell you to say. They'll fight you, but I'm with you and I'll take care of you."

(Jeremiah 1)

Meanwhile, in *your* world...

Write about a time you were asked to do something you weren't sure you could do—but you had to try anyway.

You and God...

Plant yourself in front of a mirror and study your face. God knows that face you're seeing. Knows every corner and dimple and blemish. But unlike pretty much everyone else, God knows what's *under* that face. He knows *you*. The *real* you. And he loves what he sees.

As you look at your face, thank God for his love. His over-the-top, crazy-about-you, never-give-up love for you—his much-loved creation.

You and others...

God knew Jeremiah better than Jeremiah knew Jeremiah. Show your family you know them by together playing the Name Game. It's easy: Using the first initial of each person's name, give them a compliment. Maybe "Nice Nancy" or "Sweet Sheila" or "Buff-to-the-bone Bob."

One rule: All names *must* be compliments!

Friendship Nugget

Friends build one another up.

SHADRACH, MESHACH, AND ABEDNEGO

Babylon's King Nebuchadnezzar set up a bigger-than-life gold statue of himself and expected everyone to bow to it. Why? Because he thought he was a god.

But three Jewish men working for the king knew better. They knew the *real* God— and they weren't going to bow down and worship a statue.

Would they get in trouble? Probably. *Definitely*—but God helped them stand strong.

They didn't bow to the silly statue, and

that made the king furious. He stomped. And screamed. And ordered that a furnace be fired up until it was hotter than hot. Then the king had the three men—Shadrach, Meshach, and Abednego—shoved into the flames.

That would teach them a lesson!

Except the king—watching for the three men to burst into flames—saw something he didn't expect. They weren't on fire. And they weren't alone. A fourth person (wait... is that a person or God?) was in the furnace with them.

The king called for Shadrach, Meshach, and Abednego to come out of the furnace and out they strolled, untouched. AMAZING! They didn't even smell like smoke!

King Nebuchadnezzar stood there, slack-jawed. When at last he could talk, he praised the three men. They'd had the courage to stand strong, and their God had saved them!

(Daniel 3)

Meanwhile, in *your* world...

What's a time you've stood up for God? Draw a sketch of what happened here:

You and God...

Stand up. Stand strong, as if you're ready for someone to push you off your feet. That's how it feels sometimes—like someone or something is always trying to push you down. But with God's help, you can stand strong. Tell your friend, God, how you need his help standing strong today.

You and others...

Get some friends together and create instant

action figures by drawing on white foam cups. Draw your favorite superheroes and see if you can guess who's who by looking at the cups.

Then it's Superhero Showdown time. See who can stand strong by lining up the cups and taking turns shooting rubber bands or tossing coins at the superheroes. Last hero standing is the winner!

Shadrach, Meshach, and Abednego stepped out of the fire. Then the high officers, officials, governors, and advisers crowded around them and saw that the fire had not touched them. Not a hair on their heads was singed, and their clothing was not scorched. They didn't even smell of smoke! (Daniel 3:26-27)

Friendship Nugget

Friends help each other do the right thing.

SAVING DANIEL

When Daniel worked for King Darius, the other workers felt jealous. Daniel was smarter than them. Worked harder. Got more done. Even worse, Darius was about to put Daniel in charge of all the other workers.

So the workers—administrators and officers—looked for some way to get Daniel into trouble with the king.

"The guy's got to do *something* wrong," they grumped. "We'll find it and tell the king!"

So they snuck around spying on Daniel. Peeking through his windows, they saw that Daniel prayed three times every day. Maybe they could...aha! They had a plan!

The administrators got King Darius to sign a law saying people could only pray to the king. If someone disobeyed, that person got tossed in a cave filled with hungry lions.

When Daniel was found praying, the king had no choice. He tossed Daniel in with some extra-hungry lions and waited, hoping Daniel would somehow be okay.

Daniel survived! God closed the mouths of the lions, and Daniel came out of the cave in tiptop shape. God didn't let him down!

(Daniel 6)

Meanwhile, in *your* world...

Have you ever stood up for a friend? Made sure you didn't let your friend down?

Draw or write about that here:

You and God...

God will never let you down, but you still have high and low points in your day. Get alone where you and God can talk, and tell him about a low point you've had lately...and a high point.

As your friend, he loves to listen to you talk about stuff like that!

You and others...

Like all good friends, God's got your back!

Get a few people to help you practice having each other's backs this way: Find a person about your same size. Stand back to back and lock your arms. With your arms always locked, sit down on the floor, kick your legs straight out, and then stand back up—never unlocking your arms. Ta-da!

Friendship Nugget

Friends show up when they're needed. They don't let each other down.

Jonah's Second Chance

Um...you're going the wrong way, Jonah!

God told Jonah to go to the city of Nineveh to tell people there to turn their hearts toward God. If they didn't, bad things would happen.

But Jonah didn't want to go. Nineveh was a big city, far away, in a country packed full of the very people who'd hurt Jonah's friends in the past.

So Jonah ran down the docks and hurried onto a boat going the opposite direction—as far away from Nineveh as Jonah could go.

Bad plan.

God stirred up a huge storm that sent giant waves crashing into Jonah's ship. It terrified the sailors so much they tossed Jonah overboard. A big fish swallowed up Jonah, and Jonah had three days to rethink his answer to God before the fish upchucked Jonah onto a beach. Eww! Yuck!

God gave Jonah a second chance to go to Nineveh, and this time Jonah took it. He went, the people paid attention, and God spared the city.

(Jonah 1–4)

Meanwhile, in *your* world...

Get some glue and a sheet of colored paper. Tear the paper into tiny pieces, and then make a paper mosaic of a cross below. Jesus died on a cross to give you a second chance. As you make the cross, think about the second chance God gave you.

You and God...

God gave Jonah a second chance. Who do you know who needs one? If it's someone who hurt you, will you give that person a second chance? Without, you know, the person spending three days stuck inside a fish? Talk with God about it.

You and others...

Prepare to take flight! Gather a few friends, and give everyone two sheets of paper so you can all make paper airplanes. After everyone makes one plane, see how far each plane flies. Then everyone can make a *second* plane, maybe changing the design. Toss again. Who made the best use of a second chance?

> Then the Lord spoke to Jonah a second time: "Get up and go to the great city of Nineveh, and deliver the message I have given you."
>
> This time Jonah obeyed the Lord's command and went to Nineveh, a city so large that it took three days to see it all.
>
> (Jonah 3:1-3)

Friendship Nugget

Friends give each other second chances. And third chances. And thirty-third chances. ⟫⟶

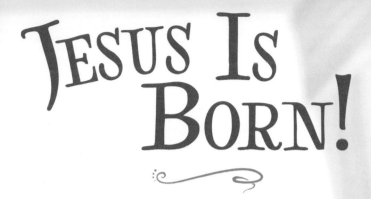

JESUS IS BORN!

If you were King of the Universe, where would you like to be born?

Jesus arrived in a cave hollowed out behind a crowded inn. His mother, Mary, wrapped him tightly in strips of cloth and laid him in a manger worn smooth by the tongues of barnyard animals.

Hardly a royal palace or regal welcome.

Beautiful angels trumpeted his arrival, but the visitors were wide-eyed, rough-around-the-edges shepherds.

They edged close to the manger to peek at the baby of *all* babies: The Son of God.

Jesus didn't see the shepherds as unworthy of a ticket to his birth. He came for just that kind of people—people who sometimes did things they shouldn't do. Who needed him. People who were sometimes forgotten. Ignored. Treated like nobodies.

He came for them—for us—because his love makes us more than nobodies. His love makes us his friends.

(Luke 2)

Meanwhile, in *your* world...

Write the names of three people you think would come help you if you were in trouble. Write their names, and then send each of them a text to thank them. Or go all old school and send them a thank-you note!

(Psst: Did you remember to put God's name on your list?)

You and God...

While you're looking at a phone, think about this: If you dial the emergency number (911 in America and Canada, 112 in Cyprus, 999 in Hong Kong), you'll talk with someone who's paid to help you. God is ready to help you

24/7/365—*for free*—because he loves you. Pick up a phone as if you're talking to God and thank him for his love!

You and others...

Play a game of 20 Questions with friends. Each of you picks a famous person—real or imagined—and answers up to 20 yes-or-no questions to see if guessers can identify the person. Who to be? Try Kermit the Frog, Abraham Lincoln, Rudolph the Red-Nosed Reindeer, the Apostle Paul...you choose!

Friendship Nugget

When you need help and someone shows up, that's when you know who your real friends are. God *always* shows up...you don't have a better friend! ⇉

> Suddenly, an angel of the Lord appeared among them, and the radiance of the Lord's glory surrounded them. They were terrified, but the angel reassured them. "Don't be afraid!" he said. "I bring you good news that will bring great joy to all people. The Savior—yes, the Messiah, the Lord —has been born today in Bethlehem, the city of David!
>
> (Luke 2:9-11)

MARY AND JOSEPH PROTECT JESUS

When Jesus was born, not everyone was happy about it.

Nasty King Herod ruled in Jerusalem when Jesus was born. He didn't like that visitors from far away came sniffing around asking about a "new king." That's what the wise men did when they called on Herod.

So Herod asked the visitors—who looked like important men—to let him know where to find the new king. You know, so he could pay his respects and maybe drop off a gift or flowers or something.

Yeah, right.

Herod planned to *kill* any new king...and God wasn't going to let that happen. God wanted little Jesus to be safe, so an angel came to Joseph in a dream.

"Get up and take Mary and Jesus to Egypt!" the angel told Joseph. "Herod is coming to find Jesus and kill him!"

Joseph shook Mary awake, and together they bundled Jesus up against the cool night air. Then, while it was still dark and the streets were empty, they left for Egypt. With God's help, Mary and Joseph protected Jesus.

The wise men—who really *were* wise— listened when an angel came to them in a dream telling them to head home without letting Herod know they'd found Jesus.

(Matthew 2)

Meanwhile, in *your* world...

Draw a picture of something that makes you feel safe. Maybe it's a person, or a place, or something that helps you feel warm and protected. And, yes, your teddy bear counts.

You and God...

If your family has a car, hop in and pull on a seat belt. That belt is there to keep you safe in case of an accident. With both hands on the seat belt, thank God for keeping Jesus safe from Herod. And thank God for caring for you, too!

You and others...

An angel came to Joseph in a dream. Do you think that's ever happened to you? Get a few friends or family members together and ask that question. Talk about your dreams.

Friendship Nugget

Friends do their best to keep one another safe.

John the Baptist Prepares the Way

John had great news to share: The Savior that God had promised from the very beginning was coming!

And not coming in a thousand years. Or in a few hundred years. Or even next year. He was coming right *now*, walking up the road there behind them.

When people turned and saw Jesus, they were seeing the Savior.

God used John to help prepare people's hearts for Jesus and his message. To see Jesus for who he was: The Light of the World. The Lamb of God. The Son of God.

People were used to going to the Temple in Jerusalem when they wanted to be near God. That's where God was, right? There in the huge building they'd carefully made to honor God and give God a home on earth.

The idea that God would come to *them*—in Jesus—was a new idea. Some people weren't sure how to think of God as a friend who'd moved into their neighborhood.

But Jesus had come—come to be with us—and John got to shout the happy message from the rooftops. Jesus was here!
He was with us!
Hallelujah!

(John 1)

Meanwhile, in *your* world...

Jesus didn't come to earth because he wanted to try the food. Or hang out at the beach. He came to be with and save people who needed him. And he still comes to be with people who need him today!

Draw a way-cool welcome mat for Jesus here:

You and God...

In your bedroom, make up a second spot for someone to sleep, as if you were having a sleepover. As you make a warm, comfortable place to grab a nap, thank God for coming to be with us in the person of Jesus. He's moved right into the neighborhood!

You and others...

Volunteer to prepare the table for a meal. Set out silverware and plates, fold napkins, make the table as special as possible. If you can, even fix the food. Do your very best to prepare as if the most important people in the world are coming... because they are!

> The next day John saw Jesus coming toward him and said, "Look! The Lamb of God who takes away the sin of the world! He is the one I was talking about when I said, 'A man is coming after me who is far greater than I am, for he existed long before me.'"
> (John 1:29-30)

Friendship Nugget

Friends enjoy spending time together. ➤➤➤

JESUS ANSWERS NICODEMUS' TOUGH QUESTIONS

Nicodemus was smart to visit Jesus at night. Had Nicodemus' buddies seen him hanging out with Jesus—that may have been a problem.

You see, Nick (can we call him Nick?) was a Jewish leader who had friends who weren't sure what to do with Jesus.

Jesus wasn't like anyone else they knew. Jesus said things nobody else said. And all that made them a little nervous. Scared, really, but they didn't want to admit that. So they got angry instead.

Nick had questions about what Jesus believed, so he went to Jesus to ask his questions. And Jesus didn't get angry or all huffy. Jesus just answered the questions...and Nick listened.

That's the thing about Jesus: He's okay with questions. So long as you're wanting to know him better, and to better understand what he says, he'll answer your questions all day long.

That's what Nick found— and it's still true today.

(John 3)

Meanwhile, in *your* world...

If you were sure you'd get an answer, what's a question you'd ask God? Write it here:

You and God...

Draw a question mark somewhere on this page. Draw two. Draw two dozen!

Then talk with God about how you feel when you have questions that aren't answered. Tell God you'll trust him no matter what—even if you don't get your questions answered.

You and others...

When people ask hard questions, they usually look right at you. So it's time for a Stare Down!

Pair up with a family member and stare into one another's eyes. See who blinks first. Even better, have family members pair up and let winners challenge winners until you've crowned the Ultimate Stare-Down Champ of the World (or at least your family).

Friendship Nugget

Friends aren't scared of asking— or answering—each other's questions. ⫸⟶

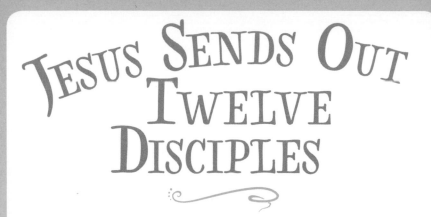

JESUS SENDS OUT TWELVE DISCIPLES

Jesus didn't give fake-smiley pep talks.

You know, the "everything is going to be fine" sort of talk you might hear just before the boat you're on sinks.

Jesus told his 12 disciples that things weren't going to be easy.

He told them not everyone would listen. That they might get hurt. But he told his

friends to not worry: The worst anyone could do to them was kill their bodies. Their souls would live on with him forever.

Jesus gave his dozen special followers the power to heal people. Cast out demons. Raise the dead. Preach and teach about the kingdom of God. Say things that not everyone liked hearing, but that were true.

Things like...people needed to turn their hearts to God. Needed to be sorry for the wrong things they'd done. Needed to become friends of Jesus.

Would it be hard? Yes—but Jesus trusted his friends to do what he asked them to do.

(Matthew 10)

Meanwhile, in *your* world...

Fill in your name:

WELCOME!
I'm:
I work for Jesus

You're working for Jesus—doing his work. What sort of stuff do you think he's asking you to do? Asking you to do right where you live... with the people you live with?

You and God...

Jesus trusts us to do what he can do, but we can't do it alone. Go to your kitchen when nobody is around and pray there. Ask God to nourish you and feed you so you can do all the things he has for you to do.

You and others...

Let's play Clone Me! Ask friends or family members whose skills they wish they could clone and have. Maybe they'd like to play soccer like a favorite star. Or be able to sing like that lady on TV. Whose skills do they wish they could clone—and why?

If you listen and ask some questions, you can learn a lot about people!

> Jesus called his twelve disciples together and gave them authority to cast out evil spirits and to heal every kind of disease and illness.
>
> (Matthew 10:1)

Friendship Nugget

Friends help each other do what has to get done.

ANSWERING A RICH MAN'S QUESTIONS

A well-dressed young man caught up to Jesus so he could ask Jesus a question.

"What good deed must I do so I can live forever?"

Good question. *Great* question—because it gave Jesus the chance to give an answer the eager young man wasn't expecting.

The man had lived a good life. He'd obeyed all the Jewish rules but knew that wasn't enough. There had to be *something* else Jesus could suggest.

What Jesus said rocked the man back in his sandals: Get rid of everything that kept him from following Jesus and then...follow Jesus.

That's where he'd find eternal life. Not in good deeds or following rules. They were okay, but only Jesus was Life.

It would be great to say the young man did what Jesus told him to do. Maybe he did, but he wasn't ready to do it yet. He went away sad, thinking it over.

(Matthew 19)

Meanwhile, in *your* world...

Who's the most important human you've ever seen in person? Draw a symbol of that person. If it was an all-star baseball player, maybe you'll draw a baseball. Sketch the symbol here:

Show what you drew to a friend, and see if that friend can guess who the famous person is— just by looking at the symbol.

You and God...

Nobody kneels and bows anymore like they did in old-timey times. Back then, the king showed up and everyone curtsied and bowed and pulled off their hats. It was all about respect and showing the king he was the most important person around.

Show God respect by kneeling and telling him he's important. That way you'll be telling *and* showing him that in your world, he's the King!

You and others...

Find out who's *really* numero uno by organizing a Thumb Wars tournament. Line up contenders and play by having two people shake hands and rather than let go, instead curl their fingers in a fist, grasping each other's hand.

Then, using only their thumbs, they'll each try to pin their opponent's thumb. Keep playing rounds until you've got a winner. Sort of. Because being a thumb war champ doesn't mean anyone's going to be bowing and curtsying in your direction!

Friendship Nugget

Friends help each other feel important. ⇛————

Jesus Talks to the Pharisees

Liars, liars, robes on fire.

That's what Jesus said—sort of—about some Jewish religious big shots who were parading around looking holy. And sounding holy.

But not *being* holy.

"It's okay to do what they tell you," Jesus said—because the big shots did a fine job talking about God. "Just don't do what they *do*. They're like pretty tombs with dead people buried inside.

The tombs look fine on the outside, but inside? Not so much."

Jesus wasn't a fan of saying one thing and doing another. Of pretending. Of doing good things so you'd be noticed. For pointing out what others did wrong when you wouldn't let God help you fix what *you* were doing wrong.

Jesus didn't want people pretending to love God—he wanted them to really love God. And he didn't want pretend followers—he wanted followers who loved him.

(Matthew 22 and 23)

Meanwhile, in *your* world...

Write down all people you follow. Maybe you're a Scout or a Brownie and have a den leader. Or you're a Lifetime Member of the Harry Potter Fan Club. Make a quick list here:

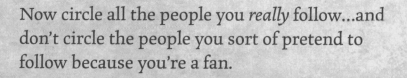

Now circle all the people you *really* follow...and don't circle the people you sort of pretend to follow because you're a fan.

You and God...

If you wrote Jesus' name on the list of who you follow, he'd love to be circled. And he's ready to hang out with you so you can know him well enough to really follow him. Talk to Jesus about that now.

You and others...

Play Mirror, Mirror with a friend or family member by taking turns reflecting what your partner is doing. If he grins, you grin. He scratches his ear, you scratch your ear. See how closely you can pretend to be a mirror and reflect what you see.

Friendship Nugget

Friends are the real deal—they mean what they say.

A WOMAN WORSHIPS JESUS

Jesus was eating dinner at a friend's house when a woman slid into the room.

She glanced around and then, picking her way through the guests, she stood right behind Jesus. She pulled the stopper out of a beautiful stone bottle—one carved out of expensive alabaster.

At once a flowery fragrance filled the room. She held a bottle of perfume—a very, very expensive one.

And then the woman slowly emptied the bottle, pouring it on Jesus' head.

It might make you angry if someone did that to you, but in Jesus' day it was a sign of great respect. The woman was showing her deep respect and love for Jesus.

Still, Jesus' disciples boiled with anger. "We could have taken that bottle and sold it for a lot of money," they grumbled. "Think how much we could have given to the poor."

But Jesus, who appreciated the woman showing him love, stopped them. "Why be mean to this woman for doing something so kind?" Jesus said. "You won't always have me here."

(Matthew 26 and Luke 7)

Meanwhile, in *your* world...

The woman who showed Jesus she loved him didn't say a word. How could you show Jesus how you feel about him—without talking?

Write about it here:

You and God...

When you do something really, really well and get a thumbs-up from someone—that feels great, doesn't it? Picture this: you've just prayed, telling Jesus you love him. You look over and Jesus is giving you a thumbs-up because he appreciates your love.

Give it a try. Tell Jesus you love him and then... see what happens.

You and others...

It's Show Respect time! The woman who worshipped Jesus showed respect by emptying a perfume bottle—something you probably don't want to do at your house. But you *can* declare this Show Respect Week at your house and encourage your family members to show one another respect...somehow. Bowing? Standing when a parent enters the room? Applauding when your sister shows up? Decide to do *something*—and you lead the way. Show that you appreciate the love of your family!

> But Jesus, aware of this, replied, "Why criticize this woman for doing such a good thing to me?"
> (Matthew 26:10)

Friendship Nugget

Friends appreciate each other—and show it.

Jesus Dies...
and
Comes Back to Life

It was a terrible, painful way to die.

Beaten nearly to death, found guilty in a late-night trial, bullied by Roman soldiers.

Betrayed by friends. Pushed and shoved through crowded streets to a hill outside of Jerusalem and then nailed to a cross to hang as a warning to anyone else who might call himself a "King."

Torn. Bloody. Alone in ways no one else could begin to understand.

And then—darkness. Death. A cave covered by a heavy stone that sealed away Jesus' body from light, from life.

Except...

Jesus *is* life. Jesus *is* light. Jesus is God—and more powerful than death.

Early Sunday morning, just as the sun rose, women came to Jesus' tomb. What they hoped to find—Jesus' body—was nowhere to be seen. Instead, an angel greeted them with news that flooded them with hope.

Jesus had risen. He was alive. And the women had a message to carry first to Jesus' other followers and then to an entire world.

Jesus had come back to life—and we can live forever with him!

(Matthew 27 and 28)

Meanwhile, in *your* world...

Forever is...a long time. A *really* long time. Longer even than a decillion years—that's a "1" followed by 33 zeroes. Write that number below:

> 1

How big is a decillion? Well, if you had every penny ever made in the United States, you'd have about 300 billion pennies—that's a 300 with just 9 zeroes. Plus you'd have a piggy bank about the size of Nova Scotia.

There's no number big enough to describe how many years "forever" is—but that's how long you'll be with God when you trust in Jesus.

You and God...

You'll be with God a very long time—so get to know him better. Find a quiet spot where you can talk out loud. Finish this sentence: "God, here's what's been happening lately..."

You and others...

Start a story with one line and then ask a friend to add a line. Keep going until someone's stuck.

Friendship Nugget

When you love and follow Jesus, you don't have to *hope* you'll live forever with him—you can be *sure*. Your friend, God, has promised and God always keeps his promises! ⋙━

> Then the angel spoke to the women. "Don't be afraid!" he said. "I know you are looking for Jesus, who was crucified. He isn't here! He is risen from the dead, just as he said would happen. Come, see where his body was lying."
> (Matthew 28:5-6)

DEALING
WITH
THOMAS' DOUBTS

Everyone had seen Jesus except for Thomas.

Jesus' followers sat huddled behind locked doors after Jesus was killed and buried. Then, BAM! There he appeared in the room!

Only Thomas missed Jesus' showing up. He found it hard to believe it had really happened. "I'll believe it when I see his scars with my own eyes," Thomas said.

Eight days later, while Thomas was around, Jesus appeared again.

Jesus turned toward Thomas and held out his hands to his wide-eyed friend. "Come see for yourself," Jesus said gently.

Jesus wasn't making fun of Thomas. Jesus wasn't mad. He was just giving Thomas what his friend needed to trust—to *really* trust—that Jesus was alive.

(John 20)

Meanwhile, in *your* world...

If you have a doubt about Jesus, write it below. Maybe something like, "Did you *really* come back from the dead?" or "Do you *really* love me?"

You and God...

Tell God what you wrote, and maybe a Christian grown-up you respect, too. See what they both have to say.

You and others...

It's not *always* bad to be a doubter. Being careful about what to believe can keep you out of a lot of trouble...like flunking a history test. See if your friends can pass this quiz:

True or False: The Pilgrims hosted the first Thanksgiving in the U.S.

False: Pilgrims may have feasted in 1621, but Spanish settlers did the same in 1565.

True or False: Albert Einstein flunked math.

False: He was always an "A" math student.

True or False: Christopher Columbus discovered America.

False: First, it was already here. Second, he found an island in the Caribbean—he never set foot on America.

Friendship Nugget

When friends doubt each other, they talk about it. ⫸⟶

GOD SENDS CHRISTIANS THE HOLY SPIRIT

Jesus' followers were packed together in a room. It seemed everyone in Jerusalem was packed together—a flood of visitors had come to celebrate at the Temple. The houses were full, the streets were thick with people talking in a dozen different languages.

Suddenly, a roar like a mighty wind thundered through the room where Jesus' followers sat. Was it an earthquake? A tornado? Should everyone run?

And then what looked like a flickering flame settled on each of them. No one had ever seen anything like it. Felt anything like it.

And then somehow they were speaking in foreign languages—languages they didn't know. At least, they hadn't known the languages just minutes before.

Some of Jerusalem's visitors paused outside the house where Jesus' followers were staying. Through an open window the foreign visitors could hear snatches of their own languages.

"How can *this* be happening?" the visitors said when Jesus' followers tumbled out of the house. Everyone could see Jesus' followers were all local people. No *way* could they know languages from three countries away.

Yet there they were—talking and glowing and excited, full of power.

But where was this amazing power *coming* from? The Holy Spirit—that's where!

(Acts 2)

Meanwhile, in *your* world...

If you could have any super power, which would you want? Why that one?

Explain here—maybe you'll get the power! Then look out, world!

You and God...

Put your hand on a light switch and get ready: You're about to turn a light on and off. Not a big deal, right? Except it's a *huge* deal! You're controlling enough electricity to light up a room! The Holy Spirit can light up you, too.

As you flip the switch off and then on again, ask God to empower you to live a life for him.

You and others...

You've got the power to make something new! Put three things you found around the house on the floor—maybe a sock, a spoon, and a can opener. Challenge your friends or family to make up a fun game that uses all three of the things on the floor. Create a completely new game!

Friendship Nugget

God's a friend who gives you power to live a great life! ⫸

Suddenly, there was a sound from heaven like the roaring of a mighty windstorm, and it filled the house where they were sitting. Then, what looked like flames or tongues of fire appeared and settled on each of them. And everyone present was filled with the Holy Spirit and began speaking in other languages, as the Holy Spirit gave them this ability.

(Acts 2:2-4)

PETER HEALS A CRIPPLED BEGGAR

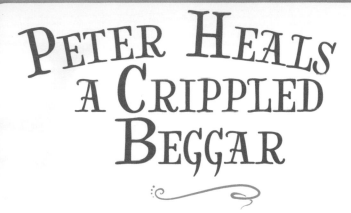

Peter and John were in Jerusalem and, as usual, in a hurry. The 3 o'clock prayer service at the Temple was starting soon, and they'd only made it as far as the Temple gate.

That's where they saw a lame beggar—one who'd been there day after day. The man asked Peter and John for money and was happy to see the two men pause.

But then Peter said something the beggar had never heard before. "Look, we don't have any money to give you," Peter said. "But I'll give you what I have. In the name of Jesus, stand up and walk."

Peter took the beggar's hand and pulled him up—and at once the beggar's withered legs were healed.

People nearby went nuts. Had they just *seen* this? INCREDIBLE!

Peter knew the men who'd killed Jesus were nearby. It was dangerous to draw attention, to stay there in the middle of a quickly growing crowd.

But God helped Peter be bold, so Peter raised a hand for quiet. "People, this wasn't us!" he shouted. "It was the power of Jesus—who you had killed. But God raised him from the dead and we know that to be true. What you just saw proves it!"

Peter boldly preached about Jesus even as he saw the Temple guards closing in, pushing through the crowd like wolves circling in for the kill.

(Acts 3)

Meanwhile, in *your* world...

Describe a time you were bold. How'd it turn out for you?

You and God...

Man, were Peter and John *bold*! They said they knew Jesus where everyone could hear. Ask Jesus if that's something he wants you to do, too. See what he says.

You and others...

Boldly show your emotions—and see if anyone can figure out what you're doing! Using your face and no hands, show these emotions one at a time and see if anyone can guess what you're showing: mad, sad, glad, scared, nervous, surprised, sleepy, embarrassed, proud, impatient, grumpy, kind, and silly.

Even better: Whisper one emotion word to each of your friends or family members and have them take turns showing those emotions. See who can guess!

Friendship Nugget

It's easier to be bold when you've got a friend by your side! ⇒⇒⇒

STEPHEN FORGIVES HIS ENEMIES

Stephen, a follower of Jesus, was a great guy. He forgave others, showed kindness, and even did miracles in the name of Jesus.

When some Jews from out of town got angry with Stephen for talking about Jesus, they tried to prove Stephen was wrong—that Jesus wasn't the Savior.

They couldn't do it, and that bugged them. *Really* bugged them. So they hired mean men to lie about Stephen. They dragged Stephen in front of the high priest.

"Those things people say you've said," the high priest said, nodding. "Are they right?"

Stephen took a deep breath and then gave an answer nobody liked. He told the high priest—and everyone listening—how all the history of the Jewish people pointed straight to Jesus.

Stephen told them that Jewish leaders in the old days had disobeyed God, and guess what? So had they. After all, *they'd* killed Jesus.

People were *upset*.

So upset they dragged Stephen outside the city gates. They picked up stones and threw the stones at Stephen—*hard*. Even as the angry crowed shattered his bones, Stephen looked up and prayed, "Lord, don't hold this against them."

With God's power, Stephen forgave his enemies, his murderers.

(Acts 7)

Meanwhile, in *your* world...

What's something so bad that you could never forgive the person who did it to you?

Scribble doodles to represent that here:

You and God...

Forgiving is hard—you need God's help. Clench your fists, hard, as you pray for his help forgiving someone who's hurt you. Then, when you've finished, relax your hands. Notice how much better they feel. That's what your heart feels like when you've forgiven someone.

Now scribble over your doodles to show God's power to forgive tough stuff.

You and others...

Stephen was quick to forgive. How quick are you and your friends? Play Penny Grab and find out!

Bend your arm so it's shoulder height and your hand is by your ear, palm up. Got it? Now balance a penny on your elbow. Your job is to drop your arm so fast that your hand catches the penny before it hits the ground. Or two pennies. Or 10!

As they stoned him, Stephen prayed, "Lord Jesus, receive my spirit." He fell to his knees, shouting, "Lord, don't charge them with this sin!" And with that, he died.

(Acts 7:59-60)

Friendship Nugget

Friends find a way to forgive. ⋙

PHILIP and AN ETHIOPIAN

Philip was minding his own business when an angel told him to get moving. "Go south down the road between Jerusalem and Gaza."

That was all. No details.

But, because Philip wanted to take directions from God, he didn't need details. He took off at once.

As he walked Philip saw an important man from Ethiopia sitting in a chariot, reading aloud. The Holy Spirit told Philip to check it out.

The Ethiopian was reading from the book of Isaiah.

"So, do you know what you're reading?" Philip asked. The man said he didn't, because there wasn't anyone to explain it. Philip hopped up in the chariot. He explained that Isaiah was writing about Jesus—and that the Ethiopian could know Jesus.

Right here. Right now.

They stopped the chariot by some water and Philip baptized the Ethiopian.

(Acts 8)

Meanwhile, in *your* world...

The Ethiopian needed some direction when it came to knowing Jesus. Where do you get direction? Maybe it's at church, or in the Bible, or...?

Draw a sketch of the places you turn to for direction here:

You and God...

If there was a fire, how would you get out of your house? That's something you can plan (*should* plan—get on that!), but you can't always plan how to get through life. For *those* directions you need to hear from God.

God loves sharing time with you, and the Holy Spirit can bring people to your mind so you can pray for them. Ask God to speak to you...and then listen. Expect to hear from God in some way.

You and others...

Invite your family on a hike to...well, you don't know. Bring a coin with you, walk out the door, and flip the coin. If it's "heads," turn left. If it's "tails," turn right. See how far you get—and where you end up!

Together, talk about this: What's the best way for your family to get directions about how to live?

> As for Philip, an angel of the Lord said to him, "Go south down the desert road that runs from Jerusalem to Gaza."
> (Acts 8:26)

Friendship Nugget

Friends come after us when we're lost and help us get back on track.

SAUL'S CHANGED LIFE

Saul was a Christian-hunter. He sniffed them out, arrested them, and then dragged them back to Jerusalem in chains.

Saul *thought* he was doing God a favor. He didn't believe in Jesus and figured anyone who did was worshipping a false god. Someone who wasn't real.

Boy, was Saul in for a surprise!

Jesus appeared to him in a burst of light that knocked Saul to the ground. As Saul scrabbled around in the dust, he heard Jesus tell him to get up, go into the city of Damascus, and wait for orders.

Saul did as he was told, but he needed help—because he was now blind.

For three days he waited, not eating or drinking anything. Then Ananias, a friend of Jesus who lived in Damascus, got a message from God telling him to go heal Saul.

"But isn't this the guy who's been doing terrible things to your followers?" Ananias gulped. "Are you sure about this?"

Jesus was sure, and that was enough for Ananias. Ananias found Saul, laid his hands on Saul's shoulders, and at once Saul's eyes were healed.

Saul's life was changed—forever.

(Acts 9)

Meanwhile, in *your* world...

Jesus helped Saul make a major-league change in life. Draw a picture of something you think Jesus might want to help you change in your life. Don't draw anything until you've asked Jesus what he has in mind.

You and God...

Saul didn't ask Jesus to help him change from a Christian-hunter into a Christian himself. But you *do* get to ask Jesus what he'd like to change in you. Do that now. See what Jesus wants.

You and others...

Get a couple of friends to join you standing on a towel. Your job is to turn over the towel without anyone stepping off the towel as you do it. You're making a change that you'll have to make together!

Friendship Nugget

Friends stick with us as we're making changes in life. ⋙⟶

PAUL and SILAS ESCAPE FROM PRISON

One day Paul and Silas saw a demon-possessed slave girl telling fortunes. She knew who they were and yelled, "Hey! These two serve God and they've come to tell you how to be saved!"

She didn't just say it...she shouted it. All day. Every day. Loudly.

Paul finally got tired of it and ordered the demon to come out of the girl. Which meant she couldn't tell fortunes anymore. And couldn't make money for the men who owned her.

The grumpy owners got Paul and Silas thrown into jail. Guards beat them and locked them in the darkest, nastiest jail cell.

About midnight, as Paul and Silas prayed and sang hymns, a bone-shaking earthquake shook the jail. Bricks tumbled down, walls fell, locked doors flew open, chains broke... but nobody was hurt. God was in control of the earthquake!

The jailer was ready to kill himself because he thought all his prisoners had run away. But Paul called out, "Don't do it! We're all still here!"

The jailer stuck his head in to check and then fell to his knees. He asked Paul how he could be saved, too. "Just believe in Jesus," Paul said—and then Paul baptized the jailer and everyone who lived in his house.

(Acts 16)

Meanwhile, in *your* world...

Look through some magazines or scout around online and come up with a picture of something you'd like God to control. Maybe you'd like God to stop wars. Or feed everyone. Or give your family more money. Paste the picture here:

Can you trust that God's in control—even if it doesn't feel like it?

You and God...

Get permission to jump in the driver's seat in a family car or truck. Grab hold of the steering wheel and hold it as you pray about who's driving your life. Is it you...or God? Who's deciding what you do? Who you pick as friends?

Ask God—and see what he tells you.

You and others...

See how easy it is to lose your sense of direction with a quick game of Spinner. Stand with your arms at your sides and have a friend or family member spin you around as quickly as possible while you keep your eyes closed. Then, when your spinner stops you, open your eyes and try to walk in a straight line.

Ask your spinner to walk beside you and catch you if you stumble.

Friendship Nugget

God's the only friend you have who can control everything. That's a great friend to have!

GOD USES TIMOTHY'S GIFTS

When Paul took Timothy along on a missionary journey, not everyone thought it was a good idea. Timothy was young—almost a kid—so what could he do?

Plenty...*that's* what he could do.

He could be a good example for others. He could teach and preach. He could encourage other followers of Jesus.

He could help people see that they needed to trust God instead of money.

To be generous. And to be hungry for growing in their faith.

Timothy could tell people who didn't yet know Jesus all about the Jesus who he served.

Too young to serve God? Ha!

God loved Paul who was old and Timothy who was young. God loves *every* age!

(Acts 16; 1 Timothy 4 and 6; 2 Timothy 1)

Meanwhile, in *your* world...

What do you think you're old enough to do for God? Sketch yourself doing it below:

You and God...

Find your baby pictures and look at them. God loved you at that age. God loves you at this age. God will love you at every age. Thank him that his love never changes.

You and others...

Everyone in your family is a different age, right? Even if you've got twins, someone showed up first! Invite your family to tell stories about the days you were all born. Where were your born? Who all was there? What was the weather like? Pull out baby books if you have them to look at pictures of your cute little selves. If you're not sure about the days everyone was born, tell stories about the first day everyone came into your family.

Friendship Nugget

You're never too young or old to need a friend!

Don't let anyone think less of you because you are young. Be an example to all believers in what you say, in the way you live, in your love, your faith, and your purity.

(1 Timothy 4:12)

AQUILA AND PRISCILLA HELP PAUL

Paul was quite a guy.

First, the Bible says he had a great education. He'd studied hard with one of the best teachers in town. He knew a lot about the Law and the prophets and how to pray and how to teach...and how to sew a tent.

The tent part wasn't something he learned at school. Pretty much every Jewish boy learned a trade at home so he could always support himself and his family.

So Paul learned tent-making. Some of Jesus' disciples had been taught to be fishermen by their fathers. And Jesus knew his way around a workshop because his dad, Joseph, had been a carpenter.

Paul knew God wanted him to tell others about Jesus, but Paul had one problem: He still needed to make enough money so he could eat and travel. And making tents was the way to go!

That was especially true when Paul met tent-making experts Aquila and Priscilla. They were a married couple who lived in the city of Corinth. They made tents for a living, so Paul joined them, living and working with them.

Hmmm...do you think any of Paul's tents are still around? Probably not—but God used Paul's tent-making talents so he could talk about something that *is* still around: the good news about Jesus!

(Acts 18)

Meanwhile, in *your* world...

Want to surprise someone in your family?
Whoever is best at sewing, ask that person to
give you a sewing lesson. Then draw the look
on that person's face below:

Hey—do take the lesson. You never know when
you'll need to sew a tent!

You and God...

Sing a prayer to God. If you're a talented singer,
sing loud. Sing like a goose honking on a foggy
morning? Sing softly. But sing out praises to
the God who has given you a voice to honor
him. And if you should happen to not have a
voice, sing through signing. He hears it all!

You and others...

Family Tent Talent Show! Gather in a room and use blankets or sheets to build a family-size tent. Everyone pile in and, all snuggled together, do a talent show. Sing, tell jokes, maybe even juggle and do card tricks. But if tossing flaming batons is your talent, you'll have to sit this one out!

Friendship Nugget

Friends share with each other—including their talents.

Jesus Is Coming Back for Us

You're invited!

When John, one of Jesus' closest friends, got the chance to peek into heaven, the adventure blew him away. He wasn't even sure how to describe it—though he did his best.

One thing he saw was that Jesus has a place in heaven for everyone who loves and follows him. And that's good news!

Jesus said this: "Let anyone who's thirsty come. Anyone who wants to can drink freely from the water of life."

That means anyone who wants to be a friend of God can become one.

Jesus wants to be with us forever. It's an open invitation.

(Revelation 21 and 22)

Meanwhile, in *your* world...

You're invited to heaven! THAT would be a cool invitation card to get in the mail. Draw what it might look like here:

You and God...

It's fun to go someplace where you're wanted. Gather up your family and take a field trip someplace like that—someplace you're welcomed warmly. Maybe to church. Or a grandparent's house. Or...?

As a family, brainstorm a spot and make it a together-adventure!

You and others...

Find a few friends and decide who you'd invite if you could have the perfect party. There's you and your crew, but who else would you have show up for pizza? It can be anybody from any time in history. See if you and your friends can agree on 10 guests!

> I heard a loud shout from the throne, saying, "Look, God's home is now among his people! He will live with them, and they will be his people. God himself will be with them. He will wipe every tear from their eyes, and there will be no more death or sorrow or crying or pain. All these things are gone forever."
> (Revelation 21:3-4)

Friendship Nugget

One way you can spot a good friend is that the person wants to be with you...and you want to be with that person. God wants to be with you. In what ways do you see him showing up?

MIKAL Keefer is a friend of God who loves God, cherry pie, his wife, kids, and grandkids...but not necessarily in that order.

DAVID Harrington's love for art began at an early age when he drew on everything, which eventually lead to a career in illustration. He graduated from the Art Center College of Design in Pasadena, where he earned a bachelor's degree in fine arts with honors. David has illustrated numerous children's books and enjoys snowboarding, surfing, and spending time with his wife and children in Laguna Hills, California.